The Complete Book of Coffee

Such taste,
For grace and joy today,
Are foretastes,
Of paradise eternally . . . . .
Sufi Proverb, 16th century

By Harry Rolnick

Other books by Harry Rolnick

A Samlor Named Desire *(Siam Publications, 1970)*

Flavors *(Siam Communications, 1972)*

Key To Bangkok *(Far East Publications, 1975)*

Eating Out In Bangkok *(Far East Publications, 1976)*

Eating Out In Hong Kong *(Asia Magazine Publications, 1979)*

Eating Out In China *(Graphic Communications, 1979)*

Reflections On Asia *(Book Marketing Limited, 1979)*

Macau: A Glimpse Of Glory *(Ted Thomas Limited, 1980)*

Eating Out In Bangkok And Pattaya *(with N. Nash , Asia Magazine Pub., 1981)*

Insight Guide To Hong Kong *(contributor, APA Productions Ltd, 1981)*

Photography by Kevin Orpin, Dinshaw Balsara, Paul Tang, Frans van Varik, Harris Gaffin and Christian Lukacsek.

Cartoons by N. Porteous.

© Copyright Melitta 1982

Designed and produced for Melitta by
Rolf Stäcker Associates Advertising Limited
602 Hoseinee House, 69 Wyndham Street, Central, Hong Kong.

Typeset in Hong Kong by
Oceanic Computerised Composing Limited.

Printing and colour separations in Hong Kong by
Dai Nippon Printing Co., Hong Kong Ltd.

Acknowledgements

First, to Shann Davies for her splendid manuscript on the history and technical side of coffee. Then to Melitta-Pacific for commissioning and aiding all phases of the book. To the Consul-General of Brazil in Hong Kong for his information. To Frena Bloomfield and Bob Walker for editing the book. And for anecdotes, leads, information and bringing coffees from far-off climes to my home, may I thank Brian Au, A. Bucher, David Butler, Donald Cheung, Tom Chapman, Danny Dubiner, Steve Ellis, Ferenc Fricsay, Janet Golden, Robert Halliday, Tada Jaiyakam, John Kikuchi, Walter Kent, Friederun Köhnen, Joseph Künzli, James Kushner, Alex Lo, Jo McBride, Nancy Nash, Norman Olley, David Perkins, Jenny and Ariel Piastunovich, Walter Ronning, Rupert Russell-Cobb, Peter Schlipf, Joanne Weinberg, Robert Woodrow and many others. Were I Spanish, I would offer my personal coffee *olé*. For this sort of book, I can still donate my personal *café au lait*. It amounts to the same thing.

Contents

"Coffee tastes so sweet. Livelier than a thousand kisses. Sweeter far than muscatel wine. Oh, I must have my coffee. The only man who pleases me is the man who presents me with coffee."

From J.S. Bach's Coffee Cantata (Number 211) words by Picander

Introduction

The love of coffee has often been compared to the love of wine — though writers usually denigrate coffee in the process. Like wine, coffee has a thousand variants. Like wine, coffee's growth is a delicate thing: a few extra dry days in the chateau region of France or the Sao Paulo region of Brazil can turn the wine or coffee economy upside down.

Like wine, coffee has inspired poetry, music and love. Coffee, like wine, has had its fanatic lovers and rabid haters.

But in the colourful histories of coffee and wine, one essential difference remains. Great wine has traditionally been reserved for the mighty: coffee with few exceptions, has percolated to the great, the mighty *and* commoner. The 1,300-year history of coffee has had its perverted figures who have tried to reserve coffee for the nobility (like Frederick the Great), or who have banned it altogether (Arab potentates and British monarchs). But coffee has always won out — and its history and preparations are a triumph for the good democratic taste of mankind in general.

If the image of wine summons up banquets, aristocrats and gourmets, the image of coffee encompasses all of these —

Coffee: The fruit that launched a trillion cups.

6

plus far more. Coffee can be the coda to a feast, the antidote to a hangover, the first drink in the morning, the ultimate drink after a fine evening.

The image of the coffee-house may summon up pictures of revolutionaries and artists, radicals and journalists, philosophers and . . . lovers of good coffee.

The image of the coffee plantation can summon up pictures of the huge lowland Brazilian *haciendas*, the volcanic uplands of Rwanda, the wild coffee-forests of Ethiopia, the lone oases of Yemen or the lush fields of Sumatra.

And the image of coffee-drinkers can summon up the warmth of the morning's first coffee, noisy noontime *Kaffeeklatsches*, solitary midnight scholars, all-night campfires in the American Far West and all-day business conferences anywhere in the world.

Wine has had its eloquent deferential poets and apologists. But coffee has had a more human, more controversial history. Coffee has been blessed as an elixir, banned as Satan's brew, praised by popes and prohibited by kings. It has been the subject of international intrigue, scholarly research, a half-dozen 18th Century cantatas and songs, an Italian comedy,

and an Agatha Christie mystery.

Coffee-house meetings have led to the creation of the Royal Society, Lloyd's of London, the *Spectator* newspaper and the English Stock Exchange. At the same time, the coffee-house has been condemned by neglected wives, greedy doctors, jealous vintners and insecure despots. It has been officially damned by Moslems, Puritans and Catholics — and officially praised by ecclesiastics of the same faiths.

Half the coffee trees in existence are the progeny of a single tree — yet every crop differs from place to place, season to season. Scientists have analysed genus *coffea* for four centuries, yet many of its properties remain a mystery.

The only people for whom coffee is not a mystery are those who drink it and love it. All those who love coffee believe that *their* coffee is the ultimate coffee, whether to start the day or to complete the night. Yet unlike wine-lovers, coffee-snobs are barely tolerated: each person looks upon his fellow coffee-lover with forebearance and respect.

As well it should be: for that simple cup of coffee, that easy and barely describable daily pleasure is the culmination of a long and frequently incredible history.

The romance of coffee

Violence, love, and the romance of a pit

Your morning cup of coffee hasn't just come from the shelf of your local market. It has come from 1,300 years of violence, piracy, tyrants, pilgrims, warriors, paramours, smugglers, poets and more than a fair share of Divine Intervention from that Great Coffee-Maker on High.

Most historians put coffee's "birth" at around the 6th Century A.D.. But British historian Sir Henry Blount hints that the ancient Spartans might have drunk coffee. How else, he asks, could one explain the "black broth" of which they wrote? Alas, there is no direct proof of the Spartan connection. And as with most of life's most valuable commodities, coffee began with a stroke of Divine Intervention.

Historians are quite certain that coffee beans (actually "pits") were eaten (not drunk) in Ethiopia and West Africa from at least the 6th Century A.D. But one legend tells how the Angel Gabriel himself came to earth to show mankind how to boil the fruit of the coffee, much as the Greek goddess Athena brought olives to mankind. But there is nothing in either the Holy Koran or commentaries which hints at this kind of intervention in the affairs of man.

Also apochryphal is the legend of Khaldi, a goatherder who, in 850 A.D., woke up one morning to see his goats dancing wildly around the plains, bleating satyr-like with the joy of the goat-god Pan himself. When Khaldi discovered that such intoxication was caused by a strange berry which the goats were eating, he tried the berry himself. Lo and behold, he found that he too was suddenly excited, clear-thinking, and abnormally happy.

Khaldi's wife, seeing the usually dour Ethiopian so sparkling, suggested that he take these "miraculous" berries to the nearest monastery. The chief monk was not only sceptical, but he threw the fruits into the fire to

Khaldi and the coffee-beans.

exorcise their power. At this point, such a heavenly aroma filled the monastery that the other monks rushed in to take a whiff. The chief monk, changing his tune somewhat, raked the fruits out of the fire and pounded them to extinguish the flames. Then he ordered them to be dunked into a ewer of hot water "so the goodness may flow through the liquid."

The date of the discovery is actually borne out by the great Arab scholar-encyclopaedist Avicenna, who, in 900 A.D., commented favourably on the medicinal value of the fruit.

But the most important story of coffee's propagation dates from the year 1258 A.D. — and it concerns the fundamental migration when coffee travelled across the Red Sea from the Ethiopian Highlands in Africa to Arabia in the Middle East.

Merchants had probably been carrying coffee with them for centuries. But the importance of this commerce was given in the possibly symbolic story of Sheikh Abou'l Hasan Schadheli, a Muslim dervish (mystic). He was journeying from Ethiopia for the pilgrimage to Mecca with his disciple Sheikh Omar. Prophesying his own death, he told Sheikh Omar that a Holy Messenger would call upon him for a very important task.

As he had foretold, Sheikh Abou died, and a veiled stranger told Sheikh Omar to dig up water from the ground. The water, said the stranger, held the spirit of Sheikh Schadheli, and Sheikh Omar would have to take it to Arabia.

This he did, taking the bowlful of magic water across the Red Sea to the port of Mocha. Omar did not proceed to Mecca. Instead, feeling peace in his heart, he settled down near Mocha, where bushes and water flourished near him. The citizens of Mocha were suspicious of this recluse, and when a plague struck the town, they accused him of bringing it upon them.

Sheikh Omar denied this. "All I have," he said, "is what you see before you." And, before they had a chance to answer, he gave them the fruit of the neighbouring tree, which he said would cure the people of their illness.

They were cured, Sheikh Omar became a noted physician and later a saint. And while Mocha today has no coffee to export, the very name Mocha is one of the most famous in all of coffeedom.

Thus, coffee made its way to Arabia. Within a few years, it had spread, with Islam, throughout the entire Middle East.

Between the 12th and 15th Centuries, coffee culture and

11

A Constantinople coffee-house.

coffee-houses were to be found between Arabia Felix (present-day Yemen) and the great centres of Mecca, Damascus and Constantinople.

For some reason, coffee was never mentioned by the Crusaders who ventured into Constantinople — either because they were thought not worthy enough to partake of the brew, or because they felt it to be merely an "infidel poison."

But it was certainly famed within Islam, both for good and evil. In 1511, for instance, noting the popularity of the coffee-houses, a governor of Mecca banned coffee entirely. (That act was rescinded later.) And in 1600, a Muslim pilgrim from India, one Baba Budan, secreted seven seeds of coffee and planted them in southern India — where coffee grows to this day.

By the middle of the 16th Century, Europeans were becoming aware of the brew. And though many were convinced that this Arabian substitute for Christian alcohol, was "unholy", Pope Clement VIII, after a few whiffs, blessed the coffee, making it a European as well as a Middle Eastern tradition. (See Chapter 5.)

Within a century, coffee-houses had opened in Italy, England, France and even in the New World. And when the Turks were defeated in Vienna in 1683, an

Pope Clement VIII, the man who laid the grounds for Christian coffee-drinking.

enterprising merchant took the beans which were the leavings of the Muslims and opened a "Christian" coffee-house.

There was only one problem: during the beginning of the 17th Century, coffee was very much a rich man's drink, a kind of morning and evening champagne. The Arabs had fiercely kept the plant to themselves; and while it was growing in India at this time, at first the only port of export was Mocha, with its fine surrounding coffee trees.

Then the Dutch intervened —

and the history of coffee was changed forever.

Actually, it was the French who first realised that they could harvest coffee in India, and they immediately brought it back to southern France to watch it bloom. It didn't, of course. Arabic coffee could never endure the frost of the area.

The Dutch were more enterprising. Dutch explorers of the 17th Century took their bean down to Ceylon (where it grew well), and also down to the East Indies (where Java's volcanic soil and tropical weather suited it perfectly).

In Ceylon, once the Portuguese spice trade had evaporated and the Dutch conquered the island in 1656, coffee became a cultivated as well as a wild plant. Comparatively little was exported until the British conquered Ceylon in 1797. By 1877, the British had expanded the coffee

Sri Lanka, where coffee blossomed in happier days.

industry, and over a quarter of a million acres of coffee were planted, yielding a million pounds a year of high-quality coffee. But in that year appeared the fungus blight which destroyed the leaves of the plant. Within ten years, the estates had been destroyed, and had to be altered for the growing of tea.

So, with the Dutch now bringing it back from two Asian ports, it became a bit cheaper for the people who longed for it.

But the major turning-point came in 1715, when the Dutch — to please the coffee-loving King Louis XIV — presented him with a single coffee tree.

They didn't know what they were doing! They knew that it had taken lot of labour to bring the Sun King the tree. They had to lug it from Mocha (where it had been secretly dug up), to Java, and finally to Holland, from where it was brought overland to Paris. But it was worth it to see Louis' face when he saw the tree. Apparently he stared at it for a day and did everything he could to propagate it in the Jardin des Plantes.

The King wanted to plant the tree in the West Indies, but the climate was unsuitable. Yet one young soldier, Martinique's Captain of Infantry, Gabriel Mathieu de Clieu, felt that Martinique's soil might perfectly fit the tree if he could get a plant for himself.

He was right — but his mission wasn't easy. First, he had to seduce a lady of King Louis' court, a friend of the court physician. She gave him three coffee plants, and Captain de Clieu took them carefully on board his ship bound for Martinique.

According to the ship's log, two of the three plants died, and such care was taken with the third that during a storm a jealous passenger actually *attacked* this last tree!

De Clieu managed to plant the tree on Martinique, and four years later he had harvested two pounds of seeds, giving them to the most prosperous farmers of the island.

Fifty years later, an official survey showed 19 *million* trees planted across the island.

The Martinique arrival with the coffee-tree.

Scenes of Brazil, a country synonymous with coffee.

The enterprising Captain de Clieu used love to obtain his beloved tree. In 1727, love was again used for agricultural skullduggery, this time by the Emperor of Brazil.

The Brazilians were very anxious indeed to get hold of the coffee plant. But so jealous were the French (not only on Martinique, but on other islands of the Indies as well as French Guiana), and the Dutch (also in the West Indies, and in Dutch Guiana), that no seedlings were allowed to be taken.

But there was one chink in the Coffee Curtain. The Dutch and the French had a little border dispute going on. So the Brazilian Emperor — nothing if not a gentleman — promised to serve as arbitrator through his friend, Lieutenant Colonel Francisco de Melo Palheta. The Lieutenant Colonel happily solved the foreign affair — and while he stayed with the French Governor of Guiana, he had his *own* little affair with the Governor's wife.

She in turn presented him with a gift: a bouquet of flowers. One of the flowers was — you guessed it — a branch of the coffee tree.

The first coffee was planted in what is now the state of Rio de Janeiro, and quickly spread into the interior of Brazil in every direction. First, the plants went into Bahia region, and by 1810, Bahia was producing 937 bags a year. Just 50 years later, it had risen to 100,000 bags a year.

In a northerly direction, Jesuit priests took coffee to the state of Espirito Santo in about 1811 — and it is from this state that the name "Santos" has come to stand for Brazilian coffee in general.

The most important states for coffee were always Sao Paulo and its neighbouring state. The spread there was helped by the availability of slave labour. Coffee plants occupied every quarter of the state and laid the foundation of a basically agricultural civilisation.

By 1836, the state was already exporting 150,000 bags of coffee. This figure had risen to 8,991,000 bags by 1900. By 1930, Sao Paulo was exporting 19,490,000 bags a year.

From Sao Paulo the coffee plant spread to the state of Parana, which today exports even more coffee than Sao Paulo itself.

Brazil soon became the king of coffee countries. But it was hardly the only coffee exporter. King Louis XIV had sent one branch of his beloved coffee tree to the Indian Ocean island of Reunion with its fine volcanic soil. That tree took root — and soon all of France was revelling in cheap (or at least moderately-priced) coffee, of a different taste entirely.

By the beginning of the 19th Century then, the Dutch were harvesting coffee in the East Indies, the West Indies and

An English coffee-house circa 1674.

Ceylon. The Brazilians were sending coffee to the New World and Europe. The Spanish were taking it from neighbouring South and Central American countries.

And the British? At first they didn't care. They were happy simply to drink it in their wonderful coffee-houses. At any rate, by the middle of the 19th Century, the British East India Company was more concerned with opium than with coffee.

But when the coffee blight wiped out Indian and Ceylonese coffee, drastic steps were taken. The British planted coffee in their East African colonies of Kenya and Uganda (ironically, just a few hundred miles from where the first wild coffee came from). Another breed of less delicate coffee, *coffea robusta*, was discovered growing wild in West Africa, and coffee plantations spread from Java to Malaya, Sumatra and the Philippines.

In *Out Of Africa* the great Danish writer, Isak Dinesen, writing under her real name, Baroness Karen Blixen, gives a good picture of a 1937 Kenyan coffee-farm. ''A coffee plantation,'' she wrote, ''is a thing that gets hold of you and does not let you go, and there is always something to do on it . . . In the wildness and irregularity of the country, a piece of land laid out and planted according to rule, looked very well . . . I was filled with admiration for my coffee-plantation, and I realised how keenly the human mind yearns for geometrical figures . . . All the country around Nairobi . . . is laid out in a similar way, and here lives a people who are constantly thinking and talking of planting, pruning or picking coffee, and who lie at night and meditate upon improvements to their coffee-factories.''

So the golden age of coffee dawned upon the world. Not only was it delicious, not only were there infinite varieties of coffee (for like wine, each coffee plant took individual characteristics from its soil, its height, its rainfall), but it was cheap.

Coffee was for thinkers, for games-players, for writers, for intellectuals — and also for the common man, the worker who wanted a lift, the American pioneer who wanted coffee "so strong it will walk away", and for the workers in the fields who wanted a drink which would keep them awake each day.

The Industrial Age produced all kinds of coffee equipment. The pumping percolator, the Napier vacuum pump, methods of decaffeination, and, in Germany, the Melitta filter system. The age of monopolies and cartels brought forth more sophisticated methods of treating coffee on the exchanges.

But through the years, coffee has never really changed its image as a magical, almost mystical drink.

It was Napoleon Bonaparte who summed it up well. "Strong coffee, much strong coffee, is what awakens me. Coffee gives me warmth, waking, an unusual force and a pain that is not without very great pleasure."

A French coffee-house named for coffee-lover Napoleon Bonaparte.

Coffee and the coffee-houses

What do the following have in common: Orson Welles, the Turkish Ambassador to Paris, the Ten Commandments, Benjamin Franklin, Lloyd's of London and Bob Dylan?

Answer: All of them have been associated with that unique, variegated, seditious, delicious, and comfortable institution, the coffee-house. And a most noble institution it is too.

Coffee-houses have engendered great films, great companies and great society. They were in the forefront of the American Revolution, European music, and in Japan, a kind of coffee kitsch. Their purposes have been political, social, literary and gustatory. In one way, all of them have been characterised by a Japanese commentator in the newspaper *Seruban* in 1935 — "The coffee-house," said this writer, "is a common living-room for those urban dwellers too poor to afford their own. It is the conference room of businessmen, and a gathering place that appeals to the nihilistic tendencies of young men infatuated by literature."

The word "nihilistic" can hardly refer to Benjamin Franklin, Voltaire, Jonathan Swift and virtually every scribe in England's 18th Century. But the coffee-house, from 16th Century Constantinople to 20th Century Greenwich Village, is an institution to be taken seriously, by kings and commoners alike.

Following is a gazetteer-history of the world of the coffee-house.

A. The Ottoman Empire

Extending from the borders of Persia down to Arabia and over to Vienna, with its capital Istanbul (Constantinople), the Ottoman Empire virtually encircled the great coffee empire. Thus it was more than coincidence that the very first coffee-house in recorded history was in Istanbul.

A statue of Franz George Kolschitzky, erected by a Viennese coffee-guild.

That fact was recorded by one Sir Henry Yule in the late Victorian Era. But the first actual description came in 1632 by William Lithgow after a trip taken in 1610. The Turks, he wrote, usually drank sherbets of water, honey and sugar. "But," he wrote, "they honour their special guests in houses with a cup of coffee made of coava bean, which they drink as hot as they possibly can."

And in 1620, one Sir Thomas Herbert came back from Persia with a rather unhappy description of a Persian coffee-house.

It wasn't only the "infidels" who disapproved of coffee. Many an irate Moslem mullah was against the coffee-house, for detaining devotees from their prayers. Sermons were delivered against the coffee-houses, and one pious sea captain, Abu'l-Su'ud Effendi,

"They sit around supping a drink . . . black, thick and bitter."

19

commanded to deliver coffee to Istanbul, secretly bored holes in his ships, plunging the cargoes of coffee into the sea.

Hajji Khalifah, a 17th Century Turkish writer, described some of the reasons why the coffee-house

The story-teller in an opulent Turkish coffee-house.

came into such disrepute. "The fact that it is drunk in gatherings," he said in his book, *The Balance Of Truth*, "passed from hand to hand, is suggestive of loose living . . . Drug addicts in particular, finding it a life-giving thing, which increases their pleasure, are willing to die for a cup." (Grammatically impossible, but never mind.) "Storytellers and musicians divert the people from their employments and working for one's living falls into disfavour. Moreover, the people, from prince to beggar, amuse themselves with knifing one another."

Which was good enough reason, according to Hajji Khalifah, for a governor of the town, Ghazi Sultan Murad, to close the coffee-houses in 1633. Of course, the closure never worked. First of all, the equivalent of the floating crap game came to Istanbul, with wandering coffee-sellers surreptitiously plying through the alleys of the town. Outside of Istanbul, there were more coffee-houses than ever.

And though, in Hajji Khalifah's words, "the coffee-houses of the capital were as desolate as the hearts of the ignorant," even he admitted that "such rules as the closing of the coffee-houses do not admit of a perpetual ban."

As to Hajji Khalifah himself, a splendid writer on food, medicine, religion and history with an excellent sense of humour, he died in 1657 — while drinking a cup of coffee in an Istanbul coffee-house!

Sadly, the Turkish coffee-house is today the Turkish teahouse (or *cayhani*). Because of foreign exchange problems, coffee is usually bootlegged in. So the old Turkish saying holds especial truth — "One cup of coffee is worth 40 years of friendship."

Throughout the 19th Century, the Turkish coffee-house was one of the most beautiful of institutions. Men would spend the long summer night sipping coffee and nibbling lovely sweet pastries like halva, and almond tarts with caramel sauce. They might play chess — but more likely they would play the most noble game of back-gammon (called onomatopoeically "tric-trac"). And they would talk business and smoke their water pipes and bargain and joke.

Coffee being a most important commodity, there was nothing minor about the implements. The coffee cups would be (as they are today in Egypt and North Africa) small, cylindrical and delicate. The trays would be beautifully ornamented with phrases from the Koran, in praise of God.

Today, in the wonderful coffee-shops of Cairo — obviously modelled after those of Constantinople — waiters will take 50 orders at a time. One may order coffee *helou* (sweet), *mazbout* (medium sweet) or *murra* (unsweetened). And out will come the large tray with all the coffee served to the right person . . . The Arabs joke, though, that all the coffee is made the same. But at the great Cairo coffee-houses, this thick and wonderful brew comes out at exactly the right sweetness and piquancy for a night of talk, jokes and backgammon.

B. Great Britain

Since the Middle East was the home of coffee, it was no surprise that the people of the Levant founded England's great coffee-houses.

The first was founded in Oxford, by a Jewish emigrant named Jacobs. So successful was he with this "exotic" drink that the young thinkers of the university crowded in each night — leading to the genesis of the Royal Society.

Two years later, the coffee-house came to London, and again it was a Levantine who founded it. One Pasqua Rosee, a Greek-Egyptian, with some financing from a merchant named Daniel Edwards, opened the Jamaica Coffee House, around St. Michael's Church in Cornwall, near today's Thread-needle Street. Rosee advertised his coffee-houses not for society, but as a remedy for consumption,

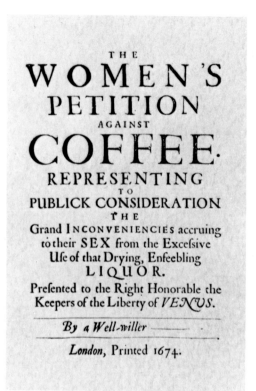

The battle of coffee, fought by the Puritans.

dropsy, gout, scurvy, "the king's evil" and "hypochondriac winds." "It so incloseth the orific of the stomach" he wrote in a pamphlet, "and fortifies the heat within, that it is very good to help digestion. It much quiets the spirits and makes the heart lightsome."

So it did. And so successful was the Jamaica Coffee House that within 20 years hundreds of others were founded. England had just emerged from the Puritan prohibitions of Cromwell's rule, and coffee-houses provided

opportunities for men to re-discover the art of conversation.

According to Frank Muir, "Many a marriage was connived, a reputation shredded, a career nipped in the bud, a poem conceived, a colleague's begarry plotted in coffee-houses such as Jonathan's, the Cocoa-Tree, Button's, and Lloyd's."

Lloyd's Coffee House in Tower Street eventually developed into the great insurance exchange, Lloyd's of London. Button's was the home of Jonathan Swift,

Addison, and Steele. Others were homes for pamphleteers and conversation of the most varied quality.

Not everyone approved of the coffee-houses, though. In the 1670s, women complained that their menfolk were spending too much time with "the excessive use of that drying, enfeebling liquor." Another pamphlet announced that the coffee-house was "a cabal of kitten critics that have only learned to spit and mew . . . and exchange, where haberdashers of political smallwares meet and mutually abuse each other."

Both the government and its opponents suspected secret cabals and plots were going on. And even the pleasure-loving king, Charles II, grew suspicious of these men talking politics. So, in a deed which echoed in foolishness only the American Prohibition act some 250 years later, King Charles issued a proclamation ordering the suppression of coffee-houses.

"They have produced," stated the proclamation issued on December 29, 1775, "very evil and dangerous effects . . . here diverse false, malicious and scandalous reports are devised."

The effect of the proclamation could have been foretold by a child. Such an uproar was created in London — and such talk of

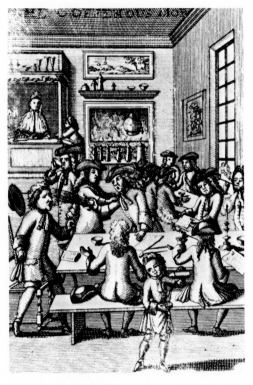

A typical evening battle royal in an English coffee-house, around 1675.

revolution against the King — that within 11 days the proclamation was revoked, and the coffee-houses opened again.

By the end of the century, over 2,000 coffee-houses were in the Greater London area, with thousands more around the countryside.

It wasn't until the middle of the 19th Century, when the East India Company was pushing tea, that the coffee-house wound down to the British private club that we know today.

23

There was perhaps another reason why coffee-houses lost their popularity. Nobody could fault the good talk and good society. But coffee during the 18th Century was nothing like the way we know it today. Instead, the grounds were boiled up with eggshells, egg yolk, mustard, oatmeal, ginger . . . and other questionable additives.

Perhaps the *reason* for so much good talk, then, was that if one was conversing, one didn't have to drink that fearful stuff.

Still, whenever one leaves a tip after a meal anywhere in the world, we can thank the coffee-house. For it was in London that a few extra pence were left for the waiter "To Insure Promptness," abbreviated to T.I.P.

Old English metal tokens issued in a London coffee-house.

An idealisation of a slave girl bringing in a tray of coffee.

C. France and Café Society

It was in the port of Marseilles, with its sailors from all over North Africa, that the original coffee-houses in France were opened. The first record of one was a seaport coffee-house in 1644. But by the 1660s, the opposition by wine merchants was so great that they were forced to close down.

Once coffee reached High Society in France — what would later justifiably be called Café Society — its popularity was so great that competitive drinks were no competition at all: they were *déclassé*.

As the home of modern diplomacy *tout de Paris* was especially impressed by the Ambassador from Turkey (officially known as The Sublime Porte). It was he, one Suleiman Aga, who charmed Paris with his coffee salons: porcelain cups, napkins fringed with gold — and, of course, what would good coffee be without slaves to serve it?

Taking advantage of the craze, an Armenian opened the first Parisian coffee-house in 1672. But it wasn't until a Florentine visitor named Procopi di Cottello opened his own Cafe Procope, opposite the Theatre Française, that the craze took off. Not only was the place beautiful, not only were ices, sherbets and other ''exotic'' drinks introduced, but the clientele included at various times Voltaire (with his 50 cups a day), Rousseau, Robespierre and Napoleon Bonaparte, who once had to leave his tricorn hat as security for an unpaid bill.

And when another regular customer, Benjamin Franklin, died in 1791, Cafe Procope was draped in black bunting inside and out.

Writing about the vogue for coffee-houses, the philosopher Montesquieu said, ''The coffee is prepared in such a way that it makes those who drink it witty: at least there is not a single soul who, on quitting the house, does not believe himself four times wittier than when he entered it.''

A typically grand Parisian coffee-house.

D. The drama of the Vienna coffee-house

There was nothing either witty or peaceful about the first Viennese coffee-houses. They had a very dramatic debut.

By 1683, the armies of the Ottoman Empire had conquered all of Eastern Europe, and 300,000 Turks, commanded by Kara Mustapha, laid siege to Vienna. The city waited desperately for word from the Emperor about their hopes for relief, but communications were cut off.

Vienna's Cafe Sperl, founded in 1881.

Cafe Landtmann, founded in 1873.

Cafe Tirolerhof.

The only hope lay in a Viennese-Hungarian merchant named Franz Kolschitzky, who had lived in Turkey and spoke the language. He slipped through the Turkish lines and found the Turks weary of the war, ready to

Below and opposite page:
Cafe Schwarzenberg, founded in 1863.

return home. With such good tidings, the Austrians succeeded in driving back the Turks, and Kolschitzky became a hero.

What did he wish for a reward? He could have had anything — but all he wanted was "A house of my own in the centre of Vienna, and possession of the heavy sacks of beans left behind by the fleeing Turks."

The "beans" were coffee, the house became a Turkish coffee-house (the Viennese were far too sophisticated to hold grudges against their enemies, not when such a good brew was waiting for them). And the Viennese coffee-house became an instant tradition.

Today, while the Viennese may "adulterate" their coffee with cream and sugar (originally honey), they have the most gorgeous cakes, cream puffs, and fruit tarts to eat with it. Names like Cafe Mozart, Sacher, Demel's and Aida are famous throughout Central Europe and beyond.

And when one thinks of Viennese coffee-houses, one thinks instinctively of Orson Welles in that Carol Reed classic, *The Third Man*. The Cafe Mozart, the zither music, spies . . . and coffee.

E. Frederick the Great and the coffee-houses

Why was coffee banned by Frederick the Great? Why should such a civilised man have written a proclamation in 1781 that coffee should only be sold to the nobility? Basically, it was because he felt that the "common people" should not indulge in luxuries. And coffee was decidedly a luxury for him. He was raised on beer-gruel himself, and though he started a coffee-house in the middle of the 18th Century, he found that smuggling was rife and that money was going out of the country. He thus banned coffee for commoners — though by the end of the century, Germany had its share of coffee-houses, leading the way to *Kaffeeklatsches.*

As for Frederick himself, he had a habit which can only be looked upon as . . . well, strange. When he was in the front lines with his troops, he would boil up his own coffee — not with water, but with champagne!

Perhaps musket powder and blood added that special regal taste, or perhaps such a brew is fit exclusively for crowned heads. But when this writer tried to brew coffee with champagne, the result was hardly imperial. For a more appealing recipe, see *The world of coffee* "Cafe du Roi".

Frederick the Great's coffee with champagne.

F. Holland and America: The coffee-house syndrome

A peace-loving people who loved their coffee (both planting it and drinking it), the Dutch had their coffee-houses from the end of the 17th Century. They were lush, quiet, civilised, and genteel. None of the "men-only" coffee-houses for the Dutch. Women frequented them as much as men, and distinguished coffee-houses like the Wintertuin or the Krasnapolsky would draw great crowds.

It was hardly any wonder, then, that the Dutch founders of New York — known as Nieuw Amsterdam — brought their coffee-houses with them to America. Actually, the first American coffee-house was in Boston, opening in 1689. But in 1697, New York had its first — the King's Arms — and soon Philadelphia also had "Ye Coffee House".

Here was served not only coffee, but beer, cider, rum and food. As in England, it was the elite of America who flocked to the coffee-houses, The Merchants Coffee House, was used for the great reception after the first

Women in a "liberated" Dutch coffee-house.

The famous Merchants Coffee House in New York.

32

President, George Washington, was inaugurated. And for nearly a century in Greenwich Village, musicians, poets and artists have received inspiration and companionship in the coffee-house.

For the political significance of the coffee-house in America, one must turn to the chapter, *Coffee and politics*.

G. Coffee-houses in the Orient

They are everywhere. Wonderful outdoor coffee stands in Jakarta, cold-coffee *oliang* houses in Bangkok, coffee with curries in Singapore and Malaysia, a coffee-house in Food Street in Hong Kong. Coffee hasn't *yet* taken the place of tea — but it's trying hard.

George Washington at the coffee-house.

Three Hong Kong coffee shops:

The coffee shop in the lobby of the Peninsula Hotel, Kowloon.

Top: Hao Kee, one of Wanchai's numerous street cafes.

Below: Martino coffee shop in Causeway Bay.

There is no doubt that Japan is the ultimate home of the coffee-house. The first coffee-drinkers in Japan were Dutch traders, who recorded having their first cup of coffee on Asian soil in 1724 (though Portuguese traders must have bested them by at least a century in Macau).

But while the Japanese couldn't stand the drink at first, by 1888, according to writer Rene Leibowitz, two coffee-houses were established in Tokyo. They advertised that their "Kahisakan" (a sort of coffee-teahouse) was to combine a European café with a Chinese tearoom.

Right and below:
Scenes from De Bruant in Nihonbashi, Tokyo.

35

In 1913, the Café de Printemps (or *purantamu*) was opened with (sigh, embarrassment) young ladies serving the coffee. And in the 1930s, with typical Japanese irony, the shops which were called "pure tea rooms" began selling coffee exclusively.

Today, it is said that there are 16,000 *kohi* shops in Tokyo alone, while 100,000 is reckoned for the country. Some are miniature concert halls, where symphonies, opera, jazz and rock music are relayed over sophisticated stereophonic systems. Other have romantic music, poetry readings

Left, and below left:
Kissako Kaiseiken, from 1919, in Chuo-ku, Tokyo.

Top and below: Koshigi in Nihonbashi, Tokyo.

Top: Café El Pico in Chiyoda-ku, Tokyo.

Below: "Poupee", a coffee-and-snack bar in
          Chuo-ku, Tokyo.

Coffee shop in Ginza, Tokyo.

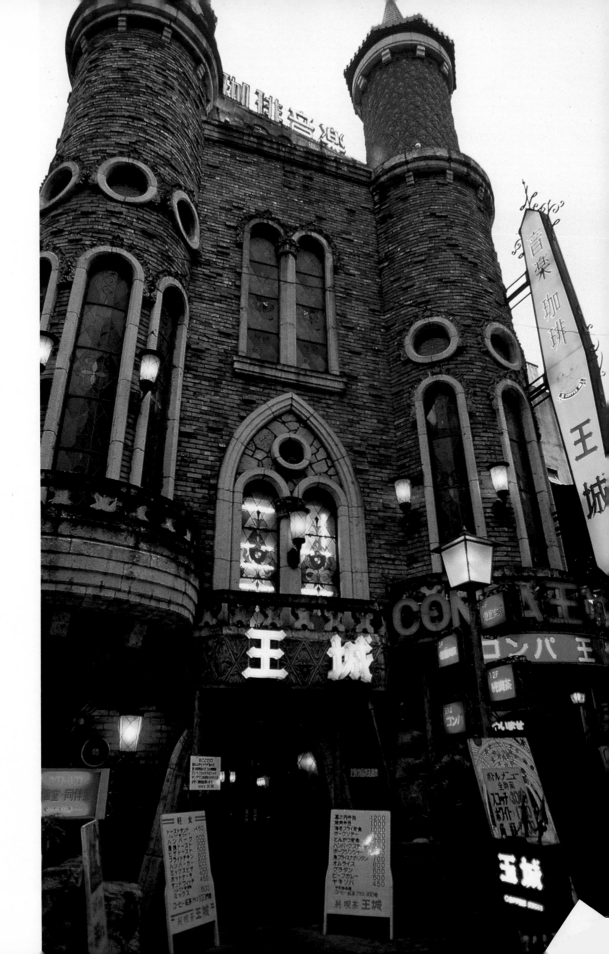

Scenes from Café Ranzu in Ohta-ku, Tokyo.

or the most opulent decor. Places like Lily of the Valley or Picasso, Hygiene, Ten Commandments (the latter looking as if it were straight out of a Cecil B. DeMille epic) and Magicland, have everything from monstrous five-storey-high stained-glass murals and Finnish wood, to something resembling a High Anglican church.

Taiwan, with its Japanese influence, has a number of coffee-shops, some serving sweet female companionship along with the black coffee. Korea has its Japanese-style coffee-houses in Myongdong district, frequently with classical music in the background. And even in busy Hong Kong, coffee-lovers take time out during spring and summer to sit around *Vini e Salumi*, a *trattoria* in Central district, where benches are set on the sidewalk, and espresso accompanies talk of the stock exchange and currency controls.

Café Salle De Repos in Chiyoda-ku, Tokyo.

Coffee and art

Alas, that coffee came to England just a few years too late for William Shakespeare, else we might have had a sonnet beginning:
"Shall I compare thee to coffee's bouquet?
"Nay, for thou lack'st the bitter *and* the sweet . . ."

But few are the great writers from the 17th Century onward who have not taken coffee in all its guises. In the field of literature, Voltaire, Balzac, Mark Twain and even the Marquis de Sade featured coffee as an object of art.

In music, coffee has reached more than the popular samba stage of "an awful lot of coffee in Brazil." Johann Sebastian Bach praised coffee in one of his most melodious and accessible cantatas (a sort of *Bach's populi*).

In the theatre, Carlos Goldoni wrote a play dedicated to coffee. In poetry, Alexander Pope often mentioned coffee and in Hollywood, coffee was ordered up by the Good Guy in the White Hat, while whiskey was drunk down by the bad one. The great actor, Sir Ralph Richardson, played the head of a coffee-packaging plant in *O Lucky Man*, and in art, coffee-houses have

been depicted for centuries by the finest lithographers.

But of course one must begin at the beginning, for the art of coffee: in Arabia. The Arabian coffee-house, like the Tang Dynasty teahouse in Hangzhou, was a place for scholars, artists and musicians to gather. And coffee was the drink which inspired them most.

They would sit about in these most ornate houses, with their water-pipes, their backgammon or chess sets, and their coffee waiters serving their brew in demitasse cups — and they would wait for the coffeeshop entertainers to visit them.

A far-seeing, almost visionary explorer, Carsten Neibhur, travelled to Arabia in 1763 and

An Arab trader leading a camel caravan of Mocha to the port.

found himself in a town well-known for being the centre of the coffee trade, Beit el-Fakih. Although Neibhur almost died on the trip, it wasn't the fault of the coffee, which he thoroughly enjoyed. And with an artist's sensitivity, he described the importance of the coffee-shop.

"These," he wrote later, "are the only theatres for the exercise of profane eloquence . . . The Arabs would find their evenings extremely irksome if readers and orators, mainly poor scholars, were not there to entertain them. These young scholars walk about and recite or deliver discourses upon all subjects. They make up the most wonderful tales, inventing, singing, making tales and fables."

This was of course more sophisticated than traditional Bedouin coffee-drinking. But the coffee ritual is so great in the desert between Syria and Iraq that the morning grinding calls for its own art. The beans are ground up in mortar and pestle, and when done carefully, can take up to 20 minutes for a few cups worth. The music created by this grinding is quite fascinating. The up-and-down grinding creates a group of rhythmic low notes standing as a kind of ostinato. Those who have finished grinding their coffee play ornamental high notes along the *rim* of the pestle, varying them infinitely. A third

factor is the voice. Rarely will there be a full vocal line, but a series of shouts punctuates the more exciting percussive sounds.

It was in the 18th and 19th centuries that coffee came into its own artistically. Painters revelled in painting scenes of the coffee-houses, its denizens lounging, drinking, enjoying themselves uninhibitedly. At the same time in England and Germany, the most elegant implements for making coffee — pots, urns and cups — were being created, and later the most colourful labels, stamps and even special coins were minted for coffee.

The 18th Century was the time for coffee's most famous musical monument: Bach's *Secular Cantata Number 211*: The "Coffee Cantata." What a splendid piece of music this is! Even that dourest, least humorous of Bach commentators, Albert Schweitzer, had to admit that this 1732 work — officially titled *Schweight stille, plaudert nicht* ("Keep silence, don't talk") — is "totally refreshing."

Bach had good reason for writing it. During the 18th Century, the King expressly forbade the drinking of coffee for commoners (see *Coffee and politics*). Thus, specially-appointed *Kaffeeriechers* (coffee-smellers) would go about the streets sniffing out offenders. Their reward was a part of the fine subsequently paid by the drinkers.

Right: *Coffee poster.*

Below: *The three ''coffee sisters''*
            (from left): Ursula, Cordula and Salome.

Something added to improve the taste.

Coffee poster of Darboven in Hamburg.

Import and Roasting.

Meyer's import and roasting coffee.

Poster for decaffeinated coffee.

An ad for Meyer's Coffee.

Coffee blended with malt.

Meyer's import and roasting coffee.

Right: Ludwig Passini's painting, "Cafe Greco," in Rome, circa 1850.

Top: Malt Coffee.

Below: Coffee and cakes at Hamburg's "Old Country House."

48

49

Top: *Open house in a Hamburg coffee-house,*
          with an all-star cast.

Below: *Oil painting from*
          Germanisches Museum Nuremberg.

A page from Bach's original manuscript for the "Coffee Cantata."

J.S. Bach.

Just about everybody made fun of such rulings, and Bach's favourite librettist, Picander, wrote a popular satire on the subject. The King, he wrote, banned coffee, so women died as if the plague were raging. Picander expanded on that (apparently when Bach asked him) and in the poem of the cantata, he told of Father Schlendrian telling his daughter to break the coffee habit. "Father," sings his daughter, "If I don't drink my little cup of coffee three times a day, I'll dry up like a piece of roast goat-flesh." In a roguish aria, she sings in praise of coffee (It's "lovelier than a thousand kisses, sweeter than muscatel wine. There's no way to please me except with coffee.") Then she tells her father that she will sacrifice everything — her fashions, her walks, her ribbons — before she'll sacrifice coffee.

As for choosing a husband, this girl makes certain that "no wooer need come to the house unless he will promise, and have it put into the marriage settlement, that I may have freedom to make coffee whenever I want."

This is the music which Albert Schweitzer calls "more like Offenbach and French light opera than that of a church organist."

But the *Coffee Cantata* wasn't the first "serious" music about coffee. Way back in 1703, a whole *collection* of cantatas about coffee was published in Paris (though none survive to this day).

Bach was just the first of the "three B's" to appreciate coffee. Ludwig van Beethoven never wrote about coffee, but he frequently stated to intimates how much he loved strong coffee. One biographer said that the composer — who paid little attention to food and whose favourite dish was simply mashed eggs — gave special care to his coffee, carefully measuring out 60 beans per cup.

Johannes Brahms, circa 1853.

And Johannes Brahms also had a special obsession with coffee. At about 5 a.m., he would wake up in his old furnished room and take out the most important materials for the day: his music-composition paper, his box of cheap cigars, and his coffee-making machine. Brahms never allowed anybody to make the coffee except himself. "Nobody," he told a friend, "can make coffee as strongly as I can."

The music for coffee didn't end with Brahms. Some of America's new poets and song-writers have used coffee in their own ways. Carly Simon in *You're So Vain*, wrote of "these clouds in my coffee." Bob Dylan wrote a sad lyric, singing,
"One more cup of coffee for the road
"One more cup of coffee before I go to the valley below."
And the very first Moog Synthesiser used in pop music came in a song called *Percolator*, where the Moog imitated — guess what — percolating coffee.

In theatre, the Italian dramatist Carlo Goldoni (1701-1793) wrote 150 comedies, amongst which the finest was *La Bottega del Caffe* (The Coffee-House). Characters go in and out ordering coffee, sending it back, calling for it to be stronger, weaker, blacker, not so black, all the while telling of their problems in fashions, in love, in the gambling house. Coffee here is the great leveller.

Then there were the philosophers on coffee. It was said that Voltaire could never have written all his philosophy without his *50 cups* a day. And when warned that coffee was a "slow poison," the 80-year-old philosopher replied, "I think it *must* be slow. I've been drinking it for 65 years and I'm not dead yet!"

His contemporary, Jean-Jacques Rousseau, was just as fond of coffee. How it fitted in with his idea of "the noble savage" is not recorded, but he called for coffee when he was dying — as he did throughout his life.

It took more than two centuries from Goldoni's "The Coffee-House" for another coffee drama to make its debut. But in 1979, Raun Raun Theatre, the popular folk-theatre of Papua New Guinea, premiered "Taim Bilong Kopi", "The Coffee Play", which has since had hundreds of performances around Papua New Guinea, through virtually every coffee-growing village. Raun Raun Theatre, founded in 1979, has a repertory company of 28, and a repertoire of nearly 20 plays. The plays are "made" by the company, either from original poems; or, in the case of "Taim Bilong Kopi",to help in a particular social problem. In this case, after some investigation, it was found that coffee as a cash crop was leading to a certain amount of injustice (from the coffee-buyers), and an equal amount of greed (from coffee-growers who kept their small crop to themselves). The drama revolves around a girl who has graduated in agricultural studies from the university. She returns to a village and attempts to teach a kind of communal farming, where profits are shared by the village. She also attempts to teach about the economics of coffee, and how best to sell the crop by eliminating the middle man.

But it is the style of Raun Raun which is most fascinating. This is no straight educational play. Like all New Guinean drama, it involves a whole series of feelings. There is a certain amount of melodrama with the plantation-manager, a rather wicked fellow; much comedy, symbolised by the clowns who dance around providing a sort of opposition to the "progressive" way of doing things; and a combination of the licentious and the ghostly. And coffee itself is symbolised by a spirit (Mama Bilong Kopi). One feeds Mama Bilong Kopi coffee in the mouth, and out of the spirit's rear end come coins!

The music is original and played by guitar, tuned in the individual manner of the villages.

Voltaire: Coffee cups and Candide.

The Scottish philosopher Sir James MacKintosh (1765-1832) proposed that "the powers of a man's mind are directly proportional to the quantity of coffee he drank." (Sir James was reputed to drink more than a dozen cups a day.)

And the great German philosopher, Immanuel Kant, who didn't start drinking until old age, was so fond of coffee that he would positively scream for it if it wasn't ready. Thomas de Quincey didn't know Kant personally, but he did write one of the *great* coffee anecdotes in his *Blackwood's Magazine* profile of Kant: "Arrangements for Kant's coffee were always made in advance: the coffee was ground, and the water was boiling. And in the very moment the word was given, the servant shot forward like an arrow and plunged the coffee into the water. All that remained, therefore, was to give it time to boil up. But this trifling delay seemed unendurable to Kant. If it were said, 'Dear Professor, the coffee will be up in a moment,' he would say, '*Will* be! *There's* the rub, that it only *will* be!' . . . When at length the servant's steps were heard upon the stairs, he would turn round to us and joyfully call out: 'Land! Land! My dear friends, I see land!' "

In poetry, Alexander Pope wrote about the dubious merits of the drink:
"Coffee surely makes the politician wise
"And see through all things with his half-shut eyes."

But Pope was surer of himself in one of the lovely , less sceptical of his verses:
"As long as Mocha's happy tree shall grow,
"While berries crackle or while mills shall go;
"While smoking streams from silver spouts shall glide,
"Or China's earth receive the sable tide,
"While coffee shall to British nymphs be dear,
"While fragrant steams the bended head shall cheer,
"Or grateful bitters shall delight the taste,
"So long her honours, name and praise shall last."

Amongst French writers, Talleyrand (1754-1838) could have been accused of plagiarism: it was he who said,
"Coffee should be sweet as love, black as hell and strong as death." Except that the Turks had said the same thing three hundred years before!

More original was Honore de Balzac (1799-1850). It is doubtful if any writer wrote as much as he did — he created more than 100 novels — and he attributed much of his success to nothing less than coffee.

"Coffee," he wrote "falls into the stomach, and there is a general commotion. Ideas begin to move like the battalions of the Grand Army of the Republic on the battlefield. Things remembered arrive at full gallop . . . The light cavalry of comparisons delivers charges, the artillery of logic hurries up with trains and ammunition, the shafts of wit start up like sharpshooters. Similes arise, the paper is covered with ink; for the struggle begins and is concluded with torrents of black water, just like a battle with powder."

Nor did Napoleon Bonaparte, whose battles existed in reality, disagree with him. To Napoleon, coffee gave warmth, force and "a pain that is not without any very great pleasure."

In conclusion, Napoleon spoke of coffee as any artist: "I would rather suffer with coffee," he said, "than be senseless."

The great culinary philosopher, Anthelme Brillat-Savarin (1755-1826) turned somewhat against coffee in his old age, attributing to it certain negative medicinal quantities. but while he gave it up in his senility, he was always just and equitable in his love for the brew. He was proud of the experiments he performed with testing coffee ground in a mill or by mortar and pestle,

Napoleon in the hands of the female coffee-drinkers: an 1810 cartoon prompted by a temporary ban on coffee to France. "Have they no grounds?" asked Napoleon. "Let them drink chicory." The ban was soon rescinded.

trying every method of finding "the best way to make coffee." And he admitted that, though "learned doctors have expressed a variety of opinions concerning the properties of coffees," nothing could be assured.

"Still," he said in his *Gastronomical Meditations* "it is beyond doubt that coffee causes considerable excitement in the brain." He also attributed the genius of Voltaire and the naturalist Buffon to coffee: "It is their great coffee-drinking," he wrote, "that gave one the admirable clarity, and the other the fervent harmony of his style." And as for people in general, "Coffee may be the sting in the mental lash which drives crowds

to take the roads leading to Olympus and the Temple of Memory.''

Of a rather distasteful nature was the use of coffee by the notorious Marquis de Sade (1740-1814). In his *120 Days of Sodom*, neither torture nor love-making begins until after morning coffee. And at one point, coffee was used in love-making itself. ''Coffee came next,'' wrote De Sade on the 26th day, ''but served in a passing strange manner. It was in the children's mouth, one had to sip it therefrom. They took a mouthful, swished it around in their mouth, and returned it into the mouth of him who'd served them.'' (The rest is unprintable . . . and probably impossible to do anyhow.)

In America, coffee was of political significance before the revolution — but it took Mark Twain to immortalise coffee in his *Innocents Abroad*.

''The coffee,'' he said about the brew served on an ocean voyage, ''had been growing more and more execrable, till it had ceased to be coffee altogether and had assumed the nature of mere discoloured water. It was so weak that it was transparent an inch in depth around the edge of the cup.''
Complaining to the captain, Twain says that the coffee is a disgrace, but the captain tolerates it. Twain takes him a cup of coffee and sets it down triumphantly.
''Just try that mixture once,'' he says. The captain smells it and smiles: ''It *is* inferior — for *coffee* — but it is pretty fair *tea*.''
(All of which is reminiscent of Abraham Lincoln's comment: ''If this is coffee, please bring me some tea; but if this is tea, please bring me some coffee''.)

Comedy and coffee isn't limited to Bach, Goldoni and Mark Twain. English coffee has been so notoriously bad that it has prompted true artistic humour. The great American comic Fred Allen said, ''English coffee tastes like water that has been squeezed out of a wet sleeve.''

But in all the art of coffee, it is doubtful if anyone has reached the heights of Sheikh Ansari Djerzeri Hanball Abd-al-Kadir in the 16th Century.

''Coffee, you dispel the worries of the great . . . you are the drink of the friends of God . . . You are the common man's gold, and like gold, you bring to every man the feeling of luxury and nobility. Where coffee is served, there is grace, splendour, friendship and happiness. You flow through the body as freely as life's blood, refreshing all that you touch.

''Oh drink of God's glory, your purity brings to man only well-being and nobility.''

The contemporary American poet,
Paul Oppenheimer, wrote of coffee
not simply as a drink. Rather, it is the
stimulus to the imagination in pre-
serving the remnants of love.

Brew

We drank just coffee in winter
that final year,
Feeling the strain of staying alert
in terror,
Guessing that a nervous enemy
was pitching camp,
Even as we drank to stay alert,
Somewhere inside our bitter veins.

For a time, the coffee saved us;
that and cold weather.
We felt a need for wrapping up
after love:

No fire, just your bare apartment,
a blanket,
And our disenfranchised bodies
that we kept wrapped
Anyhow among their enemy veins

That did no good. And tropics
rose up in the coffee,
Acres of lies, and escapes among
vast leaves,
Distortions of love and leafy
decay,
Orchid exaggerations that
bloomed with death,
Dying and rising in those veins

Ceylon's Peacock Hill Coffee Estate, as seen in 1864, and painted by Capt. O'Brien.

We kept embracing together in
your bare rooms.
And nights of talky heat swept up
and held me,
Stoic, in those coffee tropics, their
hard intentness —
These promising, like the coffee,
easy escapes,
Good ones, from the betrayals of
our veins

That pumped small deaths. But
even loving failed,
Sour and breathless, sarcastic,
and finally dumb,

Losing, before that winter's dying
fevers,
Inexplicably regretted and then
just longed for,
Like a drug missed in the mere
hot veins

Of an addict's flimsy body.
You said, ''Here's how this dies,''
And I hated the sweet coffee
realism of your eyes.

Paul Oppenheimer

Coffee and politics: The "Cup d'Etat"

It goes without saying that a commodity as economically important as coffee is going to have political influence. In countries like Brazil, Colombia and Indonesia, where coffee was once virtually the only export crop, the treatment of coffee-growers is equal to the treatment of the masses. And in countries around the world, where the consumption of coffee is as important as any staple in the diet, the price of coffee can indirectly be an indicator of economic trends as a whole. Marie Antoinette never did say, "Have they no water? Let them drink coffee!" But she lived in an age when coffee was more fashionable even than wine. And there were some who blamed the influence of coffee for the French Revolution itself.

At any rate, from its beginnings and the controversy between Islam and Christianity, coffee has held its own as a major factor in world events.

In a number of coffee-growing countries, certain injustices became part of the major motivations for revolution itself.

In Indonesia, for example, the post-Second World War revolution against the Dutch took Dutch economic injustice as the major reason to fight for independence. And there was much justification for this. Virtually from their colonial beginnings, the Dutch, realising the potential of the island of Java in coffee exporting, made coffee-raising a "culture cultivation." Which, in economic terms, meant that the Government claimed the land for coffee, and *corvée* labour was used to work the coffee plantations.

Indonesia.

This prompted abortive native revolutions in 1723 and 1733 but injustices continued as before. And when the Dutch Company (which had a monopoly on trade with the East Indies) had only coffee to ship during the competition with the British trading companies, they insisted that coffee be raised on "state plantations." The rule wasn't relaxed until 1920 — but sufficient resentment was aroused to cause the Sukarno Revolution to cite "Coffee Injustice" as being typical of Dutch rule.

While one could conceivably find coffee as an impetus in other revolutions, ranging from the Mau Mau Rebellion in the Kenya Highlands to today's insurrection in El Salvador, the only other direct influence of coffee-planting on revolution came in Madagascar in 1947.

The largest coffee plantation in Madagascar had always been owned by the French, who produced *arabica* and *robusta* coffee beans for the world market. But still, about 85 per cent of the coffee was grown by small farmers, Unfortunately, so much was exported that the people of Madagascar could rarely afford to drink coffee themselves. Their usual drink was the rather poor substitute of water in which rice has been boiled.

Of the two tribes which raised the coffee, the Betsimsiaraka people are very sophisticated, while the Tanala are known as "the people of the forest." Both of them had been exploited for centuries by the Chinese coffee-buyers, but they blamed their problems on the French, who owned much of the land, the plantations being worked by slave labour throughout the 19th Century.

When the revolt came in 1947, it was led by Madagascan officers who had been trained by the French. They were followed by various political parties and witch doctors. But behind them all came many of the small coffee-growers who felt that they had been exploited.

When they burned or deserted their plantations, they caused a drop in coffee production which has lasted until this day. The tragedy of the revolt is that it lasted one year — but the number of deaths is estimated at around 80,000. Predominant among the dead were the jungle men, the Tanala, who had left their coffee and had come to the cities to become cannon fodder.

The country's coffee production has barely survived, so great was the destruction.

But in these revolutions, coffee could have been substituted by any commodity. In the political revolutions, or just in politics in general, coffee plays an exceptional part.

The reason is simple. Coffee is not simply a drink with nutrients. It is, in the words of Dr. Gyula Cey-Bert, of Geneva's Research Institute For Food Preferences, ''a drink which warms, which sets ideas flowing and which gives a sense of security and comfort to the individual drinking it. Tea is a social drink, meant to provide a conservative feeling of being one with society. Coffee makes the drinker feel, if not *against* society,

Turkish coffee-house, etching by I. Wagner.

at least an individual for whom society must prove itself before he accepts it."

This is the 20th Century interpretation from a well-known socio-psychologist. But in the 16th Century, the Turks and Arabs were equally aware of coffee's "seditionary" values. The Turks called their coffee-houses "schools to the wise". To Moslems in general, coffee was the answer to the intoxication of Christian wines. Thus it was a powerful force.

So powerful that in 1511, the Governor of Mecca, ruling on behalf of the Sultan of Cairo, decided, after a long "trial," to ban coffee. In theory, when he discovered the coffee-houses (which had been opened by mystic Moslems who had used coffee in their religious services in Yemen), he criticised only the fact that "in these places, men and women meet and play violins, tambourines, chess and do other things contrary to our sacred laws". To add insult to injury, the corrupt Governor bribed two Persian doctors to say that coffee was unhealthy. Then he banned coffee altogether — proudly sending his decree to the Sultan in Cairo.

The Sultan realised what was really going on. He discovered that the *real* reason for banning coffee was that "it stimulated the common customers of coffee-houses to discuss the wrongdoings of their leaders."

The Governor had a lot of wrongdoings to be discussed. And the Sultan not only "repealed" coffee (comparing it to the Holy Islamic waters of Zem Zem), but investigated the Governor, discovering so much corruption that he was put to death.

Politics also raised its ugly head in Istanbul in 1623. When a governor there closed the coffee houses — again for preaching sedition — he opened up a can of worms. For the Turks needed their coffee and drank it secretly. Punishment was severe. For the first drink, one was beaten with a stick. For the second, one was sewn in a leather bag and dumped into the sea.
(See *Coffee and the coffee-houses*).

How could the Turks get around it? They simply opened "floating" coffee-houses. People walking around with pots of the brew, pouring out secret "quickies". Visitors to Istanbul today still see these floating drink-makers (though alas, the drink today is mainly tea!).

After coffee was "officially blessed" by a Pope (See *Coffee and religion*), coffee-houses boomed in England. But not for long. King Charles II, with exactly the same logic as the Governor of Mecca, decided that coffee-houses and coffee itself were immoral and unhealthy. The real reason was that coffee provoked unhealthy political discussion. They were, in the words of his ministers, "seminars of sedition." He banned coffee-houses entirely — but only 11 days later, the pressure was so great that he repealed his order "out of Royal Compassion."

It was at that time that coffee-houses turned into *real* political institutions. Newspapers were founded in coffee-houses, writers and politicians gathered (along with highwaymen and thieves picking up rumours on where the wealth lay) and soon the coffee-house became *so* important that a fatal mistake was made. In the early 19th Century, a group of coffee-house owners asked that a law be passed insisting that all newspapers originate out of their own coffee-houses. That was too much! And with the newest fad being tea from China, coffee died a fairly natural death until its recent revival.

In France, one could conceivably say that the Revolution was founded in the coffee-house. Inspired by hearty Haitian coffee (as well as talk about Haiti's own revolution at that time), people like Voltaire, Diderot and the great speakers and thinkers of France would find their common subjects of interest in the coffee-houses.

In July 1789, at the famous Cafe Foy, one Camille Desmoulins, a journalist "high" on coffee, leaped onto a table and made an impassioned speech about democracy and freedom. So stunned were the people at his wisdom and emotion that a crowd gathered, and two days later the Bastille fell, leading to the French Revolution.

In the New World, coffee played second fiddle to tea — until politics intervened. The politics were the "unfair" taxation imposed upon the British Colonies by King George III. Under the Townsend Act of 1767, essential articles were taxed beyond people's endurance. And when King George finally repealed the act in 1773, he retained the tax on tea — both on principle, and to help the East India Company. But the independent New Englanders wanted no part of this hated symbol of oppression. When the tea-clippers came over, the people resisted. In Charleston, the tea was locked up in vaults; in Philadelphia and New York, it was sent back to the ships. And in the most famous incident, in Boston, on December 16,1773, a party of about 50 men disguised as Indians, boarded the ships, which had sailed from Macao, burst open the 343 chests of tea and emptied them into the harbour.

War was inevitable.
So was coffee-drinking.

Tea-drinking to the Americans, was like approving British taxation. The Boston Tea Party itself was instigated by coffee-drinkers in Boston's Green Dragon Coffee House, which Daniel Webster called "the headquarters of the revolution." In New York, at the Merchants Coffee House, a group of radicals made the first plan for a union of the colonies. And in 1788, the United States Constitution was celebrated by unfurling a flag from — you guessed it — the Merchants' Coffee House.

Coffee was to remain the great American drink through all its wars. During the Mexican-American and Civil wars, coffee was a vital part of the rations. And in the American West, coffee was so important and so strong that cowboys and pioneers felt that they couldn't do without it. Coffee had to be strong enough to walk on its own! And what did American coffee have to do with the sophisticated coffee-houses of Europe? As usual, Mark Twain has the last word: "The average American's simplest . . . breakfast consists of coffee and beefsteak . . . (European coffee) resembles the real thing like hypocrisy resembles holiness. It is a feeble, characterless, uninspiring sort of stuff. (Not like) the rich beverage of home,

with its clotted layer of yellow cream on top of it."

Whether such a description of home-brewed coffee fits all, we dare not say. But coffee is history itself. And for that alone, we can all be thankful.

A bill-poster on a nineteenth-century American coffee advertisment, that spread the United States and coffee, westward.

67

Coffee and religion

As coffee is a product of the Middle East, both Moslems and Christians have praised it, condemned it, banned it and sanctified it. At one point, coffee was even baptized!

The Christians have never declared a "coffee saint", but in Islam some Arabs honour Sheikh Schadheli as the Saint of Coffee. There is nothing facetious in this, as North Africa is filled with monuments to saints who have done little more than won a battle or cleansed out a corrupt government.

Sheikh Schadheli, a great teacher, had a disciple named Omar, who had been exiled to the desert wilderness outside the Yemeni port of Mocha. Omar was starving, and the Sheikh showed him how to survive by roasting the berries of the coffee tree. Omar, now revitalised, ran to the city of Mocha with his knowledge of this great tree, which was growing wild. As a reward, he was allowed to return to the city where he became revered as a sage and as a prophet. His cairn is still somewhere in the desert outside of Mocha — though coffee itself is no longer exported from the city. (see *Violence, love and the romance of a pit*)

In another Islamic legend — one which is hardly part of the orthodox canon — the Angel Gabriel appeared to Mohammed in a dream and revealed the secret of coffee as a drink to stimulate his disciples in their prayer.

But for neither Christians nor Moslems was coffee the perfect answer. Quite the opposite. Although the great Moslem physician Avicenna praised coffee for its medicinal value. In his *Canon of Medicine* he said that it cured everything from earaches to eye-strain to liver problems — many Moslem priests condemned coffee as an *artificial* means for keeping devotees up during prayer time, and they banned it from being served anywhere near the mosques.

Being above all practical people, though, other Egyptian *mullahs* said that coffee — an "essence of caffeine" — was the ideal way to wake sleepy people to say their prayers. God, they felt, would hardly blame His people for how they were awakened as long as they said their prayers correctly.

In Turkey, the dervishes whirled about their mosques in Konya all night long — and they attributed their liveliness to coffee itself. One famous Turkish mystic even composed a poem to the brew: Mevlana Celaleddin Rumi (1207-1273), a founder of the dervish movement, wrote,

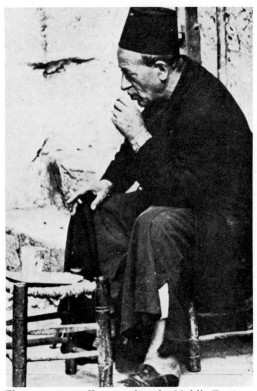
The morning coffee ritual in the Middle East.

"When the black spirits pour inside us,
Then the spirit of God and air
And all that is wonderous within
Moves us through the night, never-ending."

Mind you, not all Moslems believed that coffee was such a panacea. In fact, for a while it was banned, and only later, as coffee shops blossomed in Cairo near the mosques, was it allowed its function in helping prayer-goers in their duties. The *mullahs* did complain that the coffee-houses actually kept people from their prayers, but did nothing more to prevent its drinking after the 16th Century.

Today, coffee is very much a part of the Islamic world. Even in India, one can thank the Moslems for their "proselytisation" of coffee. In the early 1600s, an Indian Moslem who went to Mecca on a pilgrimage was so intrigued by coffee that he smuggled the seeds back to India. It was found growing by the Dutch, who re-transplanted it, first in Ceylon and later Indonesia.

Today, only the Turks have deserted coffee, as they must import it illegally. Perhaps the most touching use of coffee in the Middle East is in the desolate Empty Quarter of Arabia. Few people venture there, but one tribe — the Saar — living on the fringes of the Empty Quarter in Southern Arabia — always carry extra coffee beans with them. The great Arabist Wilfred Thesiger describes how, whenever the Saar people pass a tomb or a shrine, they leave a few coffee beans nearby. Would one consider this a religious offering? Only when one acknowledges that hospitality to the Arabs *is* religion! For inside each shrine or tomb is coffee-making equipment. And any weary traveller approaching a shrine can make his own coffee before moving on, refreshed and happy.

In Christianity, coffee has not exactly been part of the religious ritual — but rare is the era when priests, ministers or parishioners have not commented upon its divine or devilish qualities.

The latter was first commented upon at the very beginning of the Christian Coffee Era at the end of the 16th Century. The bean had been brought back by an Italian scientist (who was not averse to quoting the Moslem, Avicenna, in his medical sanctification of coffee). But Vatican diehards reasoned that coffee was not a drink fit for Christians at all. In fact, they reasoned, since the Koran had banned Christian wine, so coffee would deceive the Christians, driving them into Satan's nest.

Fortunately, Pope Clement VIII, living up to his name as a very charitable man, felt that he should try this devilish brew before passing judgement. His coffee must have been excellent, for, according to writers of his time, he positively loved the stuff.

"It is delicious," he said. "We will not let coffee remain the property of Satan. As Christians, our power is greater than Satan's, so we shall make coffee our own."

Coffee, then, has remained as much a Christian beverage as an Islamic one . . . or so it seemed for a few hundred years.

While coffee had its ups and downs politically in Europe, the English made it a frankly religious issue.

The Puritans hated it — in theory. In actuality, when the *Mayflower* sailed to the United States with pilgrims on board, coffee-making equipment was part of the important cargo. But in 1674, a pamphlet issued by Puritans called *The Woman's Petition Against Coffee*, laid it on the line: coffee-houses not only kept men from work and prayer, but, "They trifle away their time, scald their chops and spend their money, all for a little base, black, thick, nasty, bitter, stinking, nauseous puddle water."

Not exactly the most enthusiastic advertisement for coffee!

Fortunately, other writers found that coffee's virtues outweighed its supposed faults. At one point, it was felt that coffee even inhibited sexual desires. And though nobody has ever taken this seriously, the cousin of King Louis XIV felt that she should have one final swing at the poor besieged drink.

"Coffee," wrote Charlotte-Elizabeth, the Duchesse of Orleans, "is not as necessary to ministers of the reformed faith as to Catholic priests. The latter are not allowed to marry . . . and coffee, which does induce chastity, is obviously of more value to them."

Outside of Islam and Christianity, coffee has made few inroads into religion. There are some who interpret a section of the Old Testament to mean that King David was given a gift of coffee. But it would mean quite a radical departure in translation to decide that the "beans" (or in some translations, "dried beans") given to King David in *II Samuel* referred to coffee.

As for Buddhism, the only reference to coffee is *very* suspect, as it comes from a New York writer. And no matter how extraordinary Norman Mailer might be, his "religious" connotation is certainly metaphorical. Still, coffee-lovers can be pleased about Mailer's reference to the religious enlightenment which coffee brings, in his story of the first men on the moon, *Of A Fire On The Moon*. There, he describes the scene in the Apollo News Centre, which consisted of endless aisles of desks, telephones and typewriters, plus "one giant Buddha of a coffee urn."

"Coffee," Mailer writes, "is the closest the Press ever comes to *satori*."

Saunas and steam engines: The unorthodox use of coffee

What happens to coffee when it isn't looking up from the breakfast cup or merrily percolating down or bubbling up the filter? To be honest, not *that* much can be done to, with, in, by or about coffee. Songs have been composed on coffee, poems have been written, jokes have been told. The truth of the matter is that coffee belongs mainly in the cup.

But not completely.

After all, it was at least two centuries before man began boiling his coffee, and hundreds of years after that before he began roasting it. So coffee obviously had many other uses — as it still does.

Probably, the first use of coffee was in Ethiopia, West Africa and what is now Zaire, where the coffee seeds and leaves were eaten raw, long before they were drunk. Presumably, one can take the green bean and simply pop it into the mouth for extra energy. When the legendary Khaldi saw his goats eating the coffee bean, their energy came from the raw food, not the roasted, boiled bean.

But that is not the only way to use coffee as food. Sir Richard Burton (1821-1890), the most astute travel writer who ever lived, noticed several different ways of ingesting coffee in eastern Ethiopia near the Somali border.

Most tribes who wandered in the desert didn't take coffee at all, as they felt it too intoxicating. "If we drink it," a Zayla chief told Burton, "we shall want it again and again. And where can we get it if we don't have it?" However, the Galla tribe took their coffee regularly, as a food. The Galla would grind the seeds and blend them in with either animal fat or butter. Burton does not give the result (though he must have tried it). But it obviously kept the Gallas very warm in their highlands.

The coffee balls were taken by the Gallas to battle, and each ball, the size of an onion, would serve as a day's sustenance.

Other tribes in the area would actually drink a coffee liquid, but not from the bean. Instead, according to a French traveller of the early 18th Century, the shells which *enclose* the bean were taken fresh and lightly roasted over coal (never burned, simply coloured brown) and then thrown into some boiling water with a thin part of the skin. This "sultana coffee" apparently had a very sweet taste.

In Yemen and Harar (the latter now part of Ethiopia, but an independent kingdom when Burton visited it in 1855), coffee was the most valuable export, and the cruel Emir of Harar looked upon it as a jewel. He would rarely let it out of the country, hoping to keep the prices high (which they were). As for the cultivators, they weren't allowed to travel at all, lest they should "lose the art of tending the tree."

Yet the Hararis didn't drink their coffee. The berry was only for export, so they would toast the *leaf* on a griddle, after which it was pounded and made into a kind of flour. Burton mentions that in England at that time, the leaf was boiled up but not toasted. The decoction was drunk like a tea. This has apparently gone out of style.

From 910 A.D., coffee was used for medicinal purposes. This was due to the work of Avicenna. Coffee was not so much a drink as a panacea. According to Avicenna, it would dry up colds, cure coughs and unblock constipation. When dried and boiled, it would allay high blood pressure, and prevent smallpox and measles. To "dispel slothfulness," one should drink coffee with sweets and pistachio oil and butter.

But never, never drink coffee with milk: that might bring leprosy!

Coffee as ice cream doesn't go back to the dawn of ice cream itself. That would have been Marco Polo bringing "watered ices" back from China in the 13th Century. But the first actual ice *cream* was made about the time of the coffee fashion. This was mentioned in 1667, at a Knights

Marco Polo: The ice-cream man cometh.

73

Coffee liqueur.

of the Garter installation at Windsor Castle, where "strawberries, cherries and ice cream" were on the menu. And coffee ice cream has never looked back.

Unfortunately, most of the "coffee" or "mocha" ice cream served in Asia is a disaster: anaemic, made of blends of dairy mix and canned flavourings.

But in Italy, New York and San Francisco, coffee ice cream is something to be proud of. It can be made of the finest espresso, sometimes with delectable fruits, often served atop a wedge of rum-soaked sponge cake with berries . . . heavenly!

Star Cake with coffee-cream filling.

Then there are the coffee liqueurs. The most popular are Tia Maria and Kahlua. The former comes from Jamaica and it contains extracts of Blue Mountain coffee plus some spices. Its popularity comes from the days before wine in the glass was available from the bars. When a man entered an English pub, he would order a beer for himself but a more feminine drink, a Tia Maria, for his wife.

In Denmark, the Heering establishment is best known for Cherry Heering — but Kahlua has recently become well-known there. This is stronger than Tia Maria, fairly highly scented and made with Mexican coffee. A less sweet Danish coffee liqueur is Coffee Bestle.

Rarer coffee liqueurs are found everywhere that coffee is grown. In Brazil, *bahia* is made with coffee and based on a grain spirit. The Turks used to export a coffee liqueur called Pasha, but this can't be found any more. The Italians probably have several coffee liqueurs (though they prefer blending coffee with *other* liqueurs.) They export something called "Espresso" liqueur to America.

And in France, *Creme de Cacao* and *Kamok* have been known for hundreds of years.

How does one make a *Creme de Cacao*? The *Larousse Gastronomique*
gives the traditional recipe. The best mocha coffee is roasted and ground until very fine. This is infused into brandy for ten days, then distilled in a double-boiler. More coffee can be infused at this point if a stronger coffee is needed. Then sugar is added, and the liqueur is left overnight and filtered the following day.

Up until the 13th Century — and possibly today in remote areas of Ethiopia — coffee itself can be used as a wine. Not the bean, but the pulp, which is fermented and somehow made drinkable.

Coffee has been used in foods for generations. In America, the famous Deep South ham has a red gravy made when the ham is basted with black coffee. Mexican stews, venison and spare ribs are enhanced with coffee in the gravy.

Sweets are equally happy with coffee. Certainly chocolate has long been married to coffee, both in chocolate's homeland (South America) and abroad in Europe, where French chefs find it intriguing to melt chocolate over a low heat with a few drops of strong coffee. In the Middle East, dates and coffee make a genial pair. And everywhere in the world, coffee cakes, chiffons and souffles can find happy geniality with some coffee.

Finally, one comes to coffee which needs neither drinking *nor* eating.

Young woman with an old Gypsy fortune-teller, looking into the grounds of Turkish coffee cup.

In the 19th Century, coffee was used as money (or at least a substitute for taxes) during the 15 years between 1810 and 1825 in Hawaii.

Today in Lapland, the Lappish people do more than drink coffee. Traditionally, asking for marriage has involved a coffee ritual. The girl's suitor will have a "spokesman" among his retinue. He enters the house to speak with the father almost in riddles, or at least poetically. Meantime, the suitor drives around the house three times with his reindeer. If his prospective bride unhitches the reindeer, he can feel confident. But the main ritual involves coffee. The "spokesman" asks if he can make some coffee.

If agreed to, he knows that his speaking on behalf of the suitor is regarded well. The speech is finished simultaneously with the coffee — and if his words are accepted for his friend, then the coffee is accepted by the parents. If not, then he must drink the coffee by himself.

The Lapps still use coffee beans today in their game of *tablo*, which vaguely resembles backgammon. The beans are used as markers.

Gypsies around the world read fortunes through a variety of methods, and fortune-telling with coffee is not the least of it. They can tell from the grounds left in the bottom just what one's fortune will be later. (This is perhaps the only drawback to Melitta's filter method. Without grounds at the bottom of the cup, one has no grounds for predicting the future.)

Brazil discovered a most surprising use for coffee: the grounds were used as railway engine fuel! Some years ago, when the Brazilians were trying to keep the price of coffee up by destroying a bountiful harvest, they used much of it in the boilers of trains — and apparently, the grounds did make the train chug along a *little* faster . . . even if the reason they had for using the coffee was little more than a loco motive!

Finally one comes to a most unusual contemporary use of coffee. This is the Japanese "coffee sauna". Here the customers wear paper bikinis and are buried in 13 tons of ground coffee and pineapple pulp in a huge brown pool. The pineapple pulp induces fermentation, so the grounds heat up to 140 degrees Fahrenheit. One sits for an hour, and apparently the therapeutic values are good for almost anything.

One is tempted, under these circumstances to compose a Japanese *haiku*:

Morning coffee warms.
Buried nightly in the grounds,
Though, I gently cool.

What exactly does the coffee sauna accomplish? Nobody knows yet — but obviously, the sauna centre is the ideal site for people who like lots of body in their coffee!

The Brazilian solution.

77

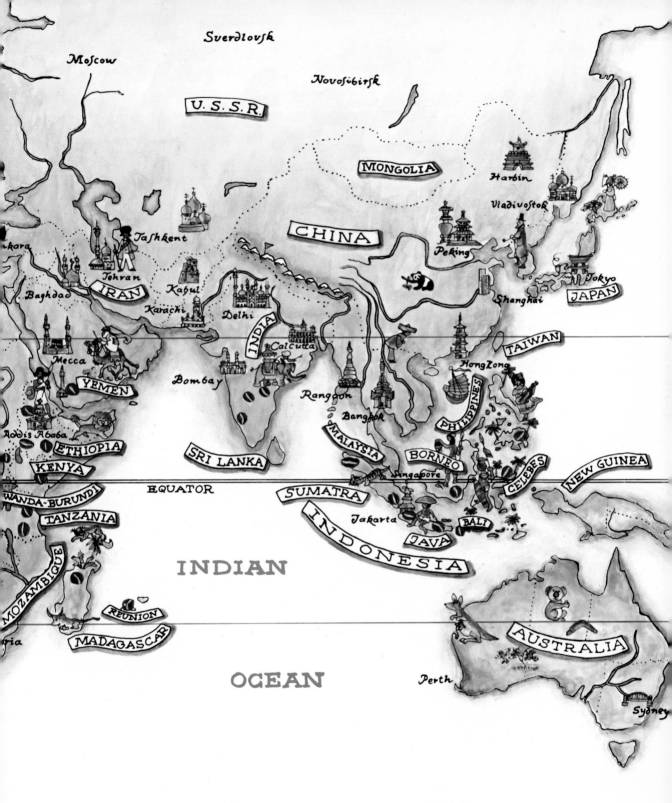

The World of Coffee

The world of coffee cups: An A-Z gazetteer

Everybody believes that *his* cup of coffee is the *only* way to drink coffee. Americans sneer at the British for their "watery brew," the English turn up their noses at thick Turkish coffee, the Arabians find that Western coffee is nothing if it doesn't have some interesting spice to liven things up.

So what is the *ideal* method of making coffee? That's like asking for a picture of the "ideal" sunset or the "ideal" dog or the "ideal" Beethoven sonata. It just can't be produced — and better is the world for such variety. For your edification then, we present some geographical varieties, in alphabetical order, on the drink which warms up the mornings of the world.

America

Apart from instant and decaffeinated coffee, America has good coffee of all kinds, brewed in every fashion. The "coffee break" is an American innovation, and has caused many a negotiation between labour union and management. It can be drunk black, with milk, sugar, sometimes with honey and spices. In Louisiana, the coffee is taken French style, with cream and sugar in the hot, heavy, black stuff.

Australia

Until World War II, Aussies confined their billy-cans to boiling up tea. But the influx of Mediterranean people after World War II generated a curiosity about coffee, as well as new coffee-lovers. Thick Turkish/Lebanese *ibrik* coffee is only a novelty (for nights out at "New Australian" restaurants). Home-brewed coffee is fairly thin. Real pride of place goes to Viennese filter coffee. Country people holidaying in Sydney make a point of "coffee-and-cake" in the King's Cross coffee-houses, and that means Viennese coffee and Viennese tortes.

Belgium

Don't expect those dainty little French cups with your morning *café au lait*. No, the Belgians prefer their coffee in big plain bowls each of which may hold up to two cups. This "*café au lait dans un grand bol*" with big lumps of sugar is accompanied by thick slabs of heavily-buttered white bread which is dunked into the bowl. The result is coffee-bread and buttered coffee, and the Belgians love it.

Brazil

Evidently, the Brazilians must enjoy their coffee for economic as well as gustatory reasons. Up to 20 cups a day are frequently drunk, and the streets of Rio are filled with coffee-carriers bringing the brew to offices. Two varieties are imbibed. In the morning is *cafe com leite*: half coffee, half milk, with an abundance of sugar. In the afternoon is *cafezinho:* a cup is almost filled with brown sugar, then black coffee is poured over it.

Denmark

The Danes drink coffee for everything: they drink it to wake up and they drink it with meals, between meals, after meals, they drink it to stay awake, and they drink it just before going to sleep so that they sleep better. The Danes also drink that fine clear spirit, *aquavit.* Ergo, the combination of coffee and *aquavit* in a touching combination called Madame Blue (named after the lovely blue coffee cups of Denmark). Here are the instructions:
a) Take a Danish copper coin and put it in the bottom of the cup, with the picture of the Monarch looking up;
b) Fill the cup with strong coffee until one cannot see the eyes of the Monarch;
c) Count to three;
d) Fill the rest of the cup up with *aquavit* until you can once again see the eyes of the Monarch. Now drink.

Egypt

The Turkish *ibrik* coffee is the usual thing — but the coffee ritual is far more impressive than in Turkey, where coffee is in short supply. Here, not a single office, appointment or buying spree can be continued without half-a-dozen cups of coffee being consumed. This is the life-blood of Cairo business.

I had an unusual experience near Cairo's City of the Dead. In one coffee-house, I was introduced to a rather elderly woman who promised that, for a little *baksheesh,* she would tell my fortune. She read neither the coffee grounds, nor my palm or head. Rather, she made me buy a *new* cup of coffee, over which she uttered an incantation. Then, I was told to hold the coffee-cup very tightly, while she prophesied all sorts of things about the future. Then she splashed out the coffee on the ground, after which I paid her for her troubles. The predictions didn't come true, I'm afraid, but this may have been because I didn't hold the cup tightly enough. One is never sure in these matters.

El Salvador

In steamy El Salvador, drinking spicy coffee is a national past-time, and they use more spices than even the Mexicans. Usually on a hot afternoon, El Salvador coffee will consist of really strong brews to which have been added cloves, cinnamon, allspice and cardamom. This is allowed to steep for an hour or two, and is poured through a fine sieve and chilled over crushed ice. For some reason, to this marvellously pungent and subtle brew, the El Salvadoreans add cream and sugar, which only seems to kill the truly artistic recipe.

Finland

The *Guinness Book of Records* once listed Finland as the country which consumes more coffee per capita than any country in the world. In 1970, the Finns drank 37.3 pounds of coffee per person. At coffee parties, at least five cups are drunk, accompanied by a wide variety of cakes and breads. One old recipe — which is still used in more traditional regions of the country, like Karelia, near the Russian border — uses fish in the coffee. As the coffee is brewing, an old piece of fish skin is thrown in, to settle and clarify the brew. When the coffee is served, the fish skin is removed.

France

A fairly bitter coffee, with the taste of West African *robusta*. Chicory is frequently added to the coffee, making it heavier, darker and more bitter. The chicory root, which looks like a turnip, is dried, roasted and ground to look like coffee. The French drink their coffee two different ways. In the morning, their *café au lait* is taken with half a cup of hot milk, and croissants. Later, people will take their morning coffee break with a demitasse of strong black coffee. The coffee is normally made with a filter.

Germany

The home of the *Kaffeeklatsch* and of Melitta. Consequently, the Germans drink more coffee per person than they drink beer. (It's a close race, though, with an annual intake of 187 litres of coffee versus 146 litres of beer!) During the time of Frederick the Great — who banned coffee for commoners — coffee for the nobility took the place at breakfast of flour soup and warm beer. Today, coffee breaks are frequent, talkative and surrounded with wonderful cakes and breads. The freshly roasted coffee is made by the filter method, usually Melitta. They don't drink it scalding hot, but with condensed milk or cream — certainly an enormous improvement on the coffee of a century ago, which scandalised Mark Twain. He didn't mind the coffee so much, but he ridiculed coffee-milk by labelling it "that pale blue juice which a German superstition regards as milk." (See also the coffee-loving, sceptical Mark Twain on Turkish coffee in this chapter.)

An 18th Century Kaffeeklatsch.

Great Britain

The coffee is not exactly strong, and many have insulted its watery contents. Fortunately, each year the British seem to improve on their coffee as their numbers increase. At the moment, it is usually drunk at mid-morning and after dinner, with milk and sugar. Poet Christopher Fry labelled it "toasted milk."

Greece

Drunk much as the Turks drink it, and drunk from morn to night.

Often cardamom seeds are added to the coffee.

Greenland

The Eskimos of Greenland revel in their coffee and, according to Lesley Blanch in her *Around The World In Eighty Dishes*, they will trade furs and leathers for tins of coffee. On festive occasions they make a kind of "eggnog coffee" with gulls' eggs. A four-cup pot of coffee is made, and about four eggs are beaten and added to the coffee as well as 4 to 6 tablespoons of sugar. While the coffee is still frothy, serve it immediately.

Holland

As the first importers and cultivators of coffee, the Dutch still have their wonderful old coffee-houses. They believe that the best coffee is the simplest coffee, served black, without milk or sugar. Usually the filter method is used.

India

Still a tea-drinking nation, India's south was the home of the first coffee outside the Middle East. So around Mysore and Kerala, coffee is still grown and drunk for breakfast and at mid-afternoon "tea-time." They roast the beans and grind them, mixing in raw sugar and boiling it all in water. Fresh milk is usually added. For afternoons, the southerners will take their snack of *dhosa masala* (a mixture of lentils, chili, mustard and onions wrapped in a little crêpe) with their coffee.

The Syriac Christians in Southwest India have a different coffee ritual. At 5.00 am, the servant will clean the kitchen utensils and prepare "jaggery coffee". This is made with unrefined palm sugar (jaggery), which is boiled in water with coffee which had been ground and roasted in the house the preceding day. The coffee is drunk black or with milk, and is the only food eaten before morning prayers.

Israel

Morning coffee is called *Kaffee hafooch* (the last two letters pronounced like clearing the throat). This means literally "upside-down coffee," and it is made by filling up half a cup with milk, then filling the rest of the cup with coffee.

Italy

Espresso still predominates (see the chapter on Brewing), with a twist of lemon peel. Sometimes, capuccino is taken with hot milk and a sprinkling of cocoa or cinnamon.

Japan

In the Japanese coffee-houses, coffee is served every way possible, and the drinker has his/her choice of milk, sugar, cinnamon, espresso, Beethoven, Brahms, Mick Jagger, Odetta or cloves. As the largest purchaser of Jamaica's Blue Mountain Coffee, Japan has coffee which is expensive but very mellow indeed.

Laos

Since the middle 1970's, when the Pathet Lao began governing Laos, coffee has become more expensive, and drinkers have less time to sit around drinking it. Then, too, the government has banned the drinking of "pure" coffee and decreed that tamarind be added, so as to save coffee for export. Still, there are doubtless little outdoor coffee-shops where one may sit at ricketty tables drinking dark-roasted brews boiled thickly in glasses with plenty of sugar and concentrated milk for breakfast. During the summer, iced coffee (*kafe yen*) is the rule.

Libya

Not only in Libya, but wherever the Bedouin still survive and haven't been lured to the oil-fields, one can be assured of coffee throughout the day. Libyan breakfasts out in the Sahara are marvellous things, even if the coffee is weak. The coffee pot will be on a glowing fire in a brazier and poured into handleless porcelain cups shaped like oversized thimbles. With the coffee comes the simple but excellent food. From a copper pot should come a creamy bowlful of *leben,* (goat's curd), followed by a black wad of dates. The date is dipped into the curd, and is followed by sips of the coffee. When the sun rises over the desert on this scene, whether in Libya, southern Tunisia or Arabia, nothing is more thrilling, isolated, sublime.

Malagasy Republic (Madagascar)

If they can afford it, the Madagascar people drink their own coffee. (Otherwise, they drink water left over from the boiling of rice.) They will usually add a few vanilla pods from their own plantations to give it a pleasant sweet flavour.

Martinique

This is where coffee first bloomed in the 18th Century. According to Lesley Blanch, Martinique's Cafe Diable consists of coffee with two lumps of sugar, a chopped bay leaf, two cloves, a big pinch of nutmeg and cinnamon and some ginger with two teaspoons of brandy. Half an orange is put in each cup, and when the orange soaks through, the brandied sugar is lit.

Mexico

For good Mexican coffee, everything except Mexican peppers is used. They take their coffee with cinnamon, cloves, sugar and sometimes cream.

Morocco

Made thickly, Turkish style, but the Moroccans frequently add peppercorns and/or salt to bring out the flavour.

Peru

Peruvians drink their coffee today like their Brazilian friends — but the Incas, after the Spanish conquest, knew how to make an instant coffee concentrate which would still stand up today. They would grow their own coffee, roast it and grind it. But then they would place the ground coffee in a pot and cover it with *cold* water. A special guard would stand over the coffee for one full day, and that night, a long involved filtering process would take place through special nets. The coffee was then drunk straight — and far stronger than any coffee could be today!

Saudi Arabia

The pulverised coffee is served with great ceremony Turkish style. Writer Claudia Roden recalls having this coffee squeezed through a filter in the coffee-pot spout filled with freshly-ground saffron pistils and cardamom.

Soviet Union

The Russians took to coffee relatively recently, after tea. And as they take their tea, they take their coffee with a slice of lemon.

Sudan

The Sudanese, both in Sudan and in southern Egypt, have a remarkable way of making their coffee. It isn't easy to find this in Khartoum, but in the villages the coffee ritual is most intriguing. First the beans are roasted dark in a special pan over charcoals. Then they are ground and mixed with cloves. The coffee is brewed by the jug method, then steeped and poured through a woven grass sieve into French demitasse glasses.

Sweden

Vying with Finland for the most cups drunk per capita, the Swedes love their coffee and coffee ceremonies. They often add a cardamom seed to their coffee, munching on little sandwiches and savories as they sip the pungent brew.

Taiwan

The Taiwanese have learned over the last five years to love their coffee when outside the home, though tea is usually drunk in family circles. But the Japanese influence is great here, with coffee-houses dominating Taiwan's nightlife. Coffee is served in dozens of different ways — and just as varied are the electronic games which are in every coffee-house.

Thailand

Thai *oliang* is the hot black thick coffee served in glasses with plenty of sugar. Boiling water is poured over grounds in a cloth bag, and canned heavy cream is usually added. Those who want their coffee black ask for this ebony brew by requesting "cafe-oh." Iced coffee is the ideal summer drink.

Turkey

The *ibrik* coffee method is described in the chapter on brewing. Unfortunately, a recent knowledgeable visitor, Ethel A. Starbird, of the *National Geographic* Senior Staff, avers that the only coffee left in Turkey is in bootleg form, brought in by the "guest workers" from Europe. The coffee is expensive, and a little less thick than the brew which Mark Twain described in his *Innocents Abroad*: "He (the servant) brought the world-renowned Turkish coffee about which poets have sung so rapturously for many generations. . . . . It was . . . . . a fraud. Of all the unchristian beverages that ever passed my lips, Turkish coffee is the worst. The cup is small, it is smeared with grounds; the coffee is black, thick, unsavory of smell and execrable taste. The bottom of the cup has a muddy sediment in it half an inch deep. This goes down your throat, and portions of it lodge by the way and produce a tickling aggravation that keeps you barking and coughing for an hour."

Traditionally, Turkish men could divorce their wives if their wives didn't keep an adequate supply in the house!

Zanzibar

Black coffee from mainland Tanzania isn't good coffee unless the Zanzibari has a handful of cloves which he munches while drinking.

87

The making of coffee

The coffee plant: Mystery and medicine

First, coffee isn't a bean. The popularly-labelled "bean" is actually the *pit* of a fruit which looks something like a cherry, although it isn't actually related to the cherry at all. And while scientists have been analysing genus *coffea* for over one thousand years, ever since Avicenna published his annals of medicine, many of its properties *still* remain a mystery.

What is this "bean", this "pit", this flowering shrub which smells on the tree like jasmine, which can be eaten, drunk, boiled, roasted, ground to a pulp, and which can turn economics upside-down?

Simply enough, the coffee plant is an evergreen shrub. It can grow in your backyard as easily — or with as much difficulty — as it grows on the lowlands of Brazil. Though it's doubtful if your coffee plant's flavour will come near to that of Brazil.

Officially, though the coffee plant has been erroneously labelled dozens of times, it is one of the 350 categories of the genus *ruiacea*, which is related to the dye, madder, and the blossoming gardenia.

Unofficially, coffee is in a class by itself. For the record, there are three major different categories of coffee, each with its own assets and defects. And no matter how each country grades its coffee, this is probably the most important label.

A. Coffea arabica

Erroneously called "arabica" by the botanist Linneaus, because he thought that the coffee grew originally in southern Arabia, which was close enough. Its heartland was Ethiopia, where it still grows.

Coffea arabica is by far the most widely-cultivated coffee: The king of coffee, which makes up 75 percent of all commercial coffees sold.

Coffea arabica, which grows wild in the mountainous rain-forests of Ethiopia, is grown throughout Indonesia, East Africa and South America (where it is somewhat arbitrarily divided into "Brazils" and "mild"). It has the advantage of being richer, tastier and more aromatic; it usually contains less moisture and has far more flavour, and usually grows a harder bean than other types.

It also has the advantage of pollinating itself (which means fewer mutations and fewer variations over the years). But like all thoroughbreds, *Coffea arabica* needs very special care. It must grow on hillsides above 3,000 feet — and 5,000 feet high is ideal. With frost, it will die. But it can't take extremes of heat either (about 17-20 degrees C, or 65-70 degrees F is ideal). The rainfall should be between 1,000-2,000 mm per square metre annually, with a peak wet season, moderate wind and high humidity. It needs well-drained volcanic soil, two hours of sunshine a day, and shade from other trees, whether by cloud cover (as in Hawaii), by trellises (as in Brazil) or by naturally larger trees (as in Ethiopia).

And all of that means that *Coffea arabica* is susceptible to all sorts of diseases. So in the 1870's, when most of the trees were wiped out throughout Asia, coffee-growers grew desperate. They needed another kind of coffee plant which wasn't so temperamental.

B. Coffea robusta

Coffea robusta was exactly what the growers wanted. In the 1870s, as if by providence, a Belgian scientist named Emile Laurant discovered the wild "robust" coffee tree growing in the Congo. Later it was discovered in the same neighbourhood, in Uganda and Rwanda.

The main advantage of *robusta* — which still grows mainly in Africa — is that it is more resistant to disease and will grow successfully at lower altitudes than *arabica*. All of the requirements of *arabica* — two hours of sunlight, volcanic soil and so on — are needed by *robusta*. But, because of its flexibility and the fact that it can be grown even below 3,000 feet, *robusta* is easier to cultivate and less temperamental.

It has only two disadvantages. First, it is not self-propagating, but depends upon pollination through wind or insects. Second, the flavour is rarely anywhere near that of good *arabica*.

True, *robusta* blends in well with *arabica*. But this means that cheaper coffees will have more than 50 percent *robusta* beans — and the cheapest will have all *robusta*.

C. Coffea liberica / Coffea excelsa

At the same time that *Coffea robusta* was found growing wild in central Africa, these two species of coffee plant were found on the west coast of Africa, around Liberia. They are the toughest and least tasty of the coffee plants. They are almost immune to disease, they flower frequently, they can grow even at sea level, or in the most difficult climes: Java, Malaysia, Philippines, Madagascar. But they are mainly consumed locally, or find their way into instant coffee blends. Tough, yes, but not very tasty.

To this could be added three varieties of some importance. *Maragogipe* is a kind of *arabica* with a large bean. Originally a Brazilian mutant, it has since gone around the world. There are so many different varieties of the *maragogipe* that it obviously takes on more regional qualities than its "maragogipe-ish" qualities.

The *peaberry* or *caracol* is a small one-seed bean, which also assumes regional characteristics.

Aged coffee is, as its name would have it, a green coffee sometimes held for six or seven years in well-ventilated warehouses. When drunk (usually in a blend), it has a syrupy richness which appeals to few except those who loathe acidity in their coffee.

What *arabica* and *robusta* have in common is a basic botanical history. Apart from the "wild" plants, one can only see these plants on a *finca* (the Spanish word for plantation), a *hacienda* (the Portuguese-Brazilian plantation) or an African plantation.

The shrubs are kept originally in a nursery, living in seed beds. Later, when a few inches high, they are transferred to pots. And after a year, when a foot high, they are taken out and planted in rows about ten feet apart, as in an apple orchard. If allowed to,

Top: Coffee shoot.

Centre: Planting.

Bottom: Coffee nursery.

Flowering coffee branch.

they would grow naturally up to 25 feet, but are pruned down to 12-15 feet.

It takes about five years before a tree can bear fruit — but the better breeds, closest to the equator, can usually bear fruit several times a year.

At the beginning of the bearing season, there is a profusion of exquisitely fragrant, five-petalled white flowers that resemble orange blossoms, but smell of jasmine. Later the cherry-like fruit appears. First it is green, then six months later it turns red and is ready for the picking.

Baroness Karen Blixen refers to the "delicate slightly bitter scent, like the blackthorn blossom." She writes about "the times of great beauty on a coffee-farm. When the plantation flowered in the beginning of the rains, it was a radiant sight, like a cloud of chalk, in the mist and the drizzling rain, over six-hundred acres of land . . . When the field reddened with the ripe berries, all the women and the children, whom they call the Totos, were called out to pick the coffee off the trees with the men; then the waggons and carts brought it down to the factory near the river."

The flowers last only a few days, and the plant may bear different fruits growing a few days apart in tight formation. It isn't rare to see white flowers, red and green fruits all on one branch.

Until recently, then, it has been impossible to have machine-picking. Coffee-picking is very much a labour-intensive job, for only experience can tell which berries to pick, which will be ready for "curing." True, mechanical coffee-pickers something like a grape harvester are used,

Harvesting the coffee.

Guatemalan coffee harvesters.

with the machine straddling the tree rows like a platform on stilts. And on the largest plantations — some of them with over a million coffee trees — this machine is at work. But there are some who say that much of the economic unrest in Central America is due to this displacing of labour, which has been halved in the past 20 years.

The yields of the trees vary widely from country to country, grade to grade. But basically, *arabica* produces 340-450 kilos per hectare, *liberica* produces 25 percent more, and *robusta* can produce up to 1,000 kilos per hectare. (One kilo of *arabica* coffee needs 2,640 dry seeds, *robusta* is 3,250, and *liberica*, the least tasty, needs only 1,760.)

One would like to think that coffee can be regulated well, most ideally, from the above description. If that were true, then everybody from the grower to the consumer would be happy. But it doesn't work so easily. While

95

there are numerous reasons for the ping-pong annual prices for coffee (see *Coffee marketing*), disease is hardly the least important, especially with sensitive *arabica*. During the growing season, the farmer must watch for leaf rust, insects (the coffee bean-borer or the infamous Mediterranean fruit fly), various root diseases and common pests.

But once the cherries blossom, the tree can yield forth many variations: some trees produce as little as 200 grams of green beans annually. Others average over three times as many.

The main figure to remember is that the annual average yield of a coffee tree is about 450 grams — *so one pound of coffee bought in a shop is the total of one tree's produce for a year.*

A tree can bloom for up to 50 years, but the best crops can be expected between the fifth and 15th year.

As for the longevity of a coffee plantation . . . this depends upon everything from insecticides to war to frost to world prices to local government policies.

Once the cherry is picked, it will be a long time before the coffee even reaches the roasting plant. And for this, one must understand the fruit.

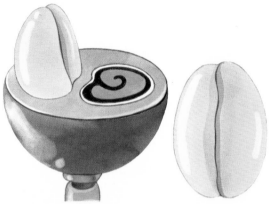

Cross-section of coffee-cherry.

First is the outer skin. Inside that is a layer of sweet pulp. The third layer is a thin parchment-like shell surrounding each of two beans. Finally, one reaches the pit: known in the trade before roasting as "green coffee."

Before any of the coffee is even taken to the port, it must be cured and the pit extracted. This can be done either with "the dry method", as in Brazil, or the "wet method" in more humid climes.

Hulling machine.

For the latter, the ripe cherries are hulled mechanically, and the bean in its parchment shell is fermented for one to two days. Then it is poured into sluiceways and washed, dried, the parchment is milled off and the bean is shipped to the seaport in grass or burlap bags. (The bags weigh 132 pounds in Brazil, 154 pounds in other countries.)

The "dry method" takes longer. The ripe cherries are spread out on concrete patios, then dried in the sun for 15—20 days, turned a few times each day to ensure even drying. After this time, the dry cherries are hulled by machine to remove the dried husk and inner skin. Then the green beans are graded according to size and shape.

Washing the coffee.

Drying the coffee.

Hand grading.

Top: Loading.

Below: Warehouse.

Once the pits are extracted, they go on a long journey — but this journey, if handled carefully, does nothing to alter the quality of the bean.

It is important to remember that unroasted beans hardly change at all during lengthy storage, if properly protected from strong odours. (The beans absorb odours.) Once roasted, though, they begin to deteriorate.

98

Ready for export.

Below: Unloading.

The unroasted beans go on a long trip from the drying ground or cleaning plant, to the railroad station or on a truck to the port. There they wait in a warehouse until the ship comes in. From shipping port to the market port may take a few weeks, after which the beans may be laid out for prospective buyers at the market. (Though with just a relatively few companies buying most of the beans, they are often transferred directly to the warehouse.)

Finally, from the warehouse, the beans will be taken to the roasting plant — and now we are on the final steps to having that Holy Grail of the morning light: the Perfect Cup of Coffee!

"In the early morning, while it was still dark and I was lying in bed, I heard the waggons loaded high up with coffee-sacks, 12 to a ton, with 16 oxen in each waggon starting on their way to Nairobi railway station up the long factory hill, with much shouting and rattling, the drivers running beside the waggons. The coffee would be on the sea in a day or two, and we could only hope for good luck at the big auction-sales in London."

Baroness Karen Blixen. "Out of Africa" (1937)

Coffee marketing: Merchants and madness

In the "primitive" days of the mid-19th Century, coffee merchants roamed the streets of New York asking coffee-house owners how much they would pay for coffee. At the end of the day, they would just sell their supplies to the highest bidder.

And to corner the market, speculators would simply go down to the coffee warehouses and buy up all the coffee in one day. Since shipping schedules were non-existent, and since nobody knew when the next coffee boat would be in town from Brazil, the retailers were at the mercy of these speculators.

That was more than a century ago — but today, the entire coffee merchandising business has, if anything, *regressed* in sophistication. In spite of agreements, pacts, agricultural experts, official exchanges and electronic information available, coffee merchandising still relies virtually entirely on fate.

"We have," said a Hong Kong commodities expert with one of the world's largest stockbrokers, "a man in New York who knows everything about coffee. He can tell you about cycles and weather, prices in 1897, and production figures for Rwanda. He can tell the difference between Java and Sumatra coffee by one sniff, and he can recite every known fact on roasting.

"But can he predict the price of coffee for next week? Or tomorrow? No way!"

Certainly in the history of coffee merchandisers, businessmen, growers and governments (who depend on the revenue) have *tried* to fix prices. Considering that the coffee business is second only to oil in revenue (at about US$2.00 per pound, one could estimate the 1980 revenue to be around US$14 billion dollars), and that it employs over 25 *million* people in dozens of countries around the world, coffee is obviously a very volatile commodity.

But trying to actually regulate prices is impossible.

The first time regulation was tried, in the 12th Century, it failed. The Arabs felt that by hoarding the seeds, by not allowing any of them out of the country, they could regulate their own prices to the coffee-houses of Constantinople and Damascus.

They didn't have a chance. An

Indian pilgrim to Mecca simply secreted seven seeds in his robes, planted them in Mysore State, and the coffee tree was already on its way to the international market.

Later, when Frederick the Great saw the coffers of his State being emptied on this "wasteful drink," he made a partial ban. Once again a failure.

If regulations were failures, pure greed once totally destroyed a whole economy. According to Compton Mackenzie in *Realms Of Silver*, the history of the Chartered Bank, when the coffee-pest first struck Ceylonese coffee in the 1870's, coffee-growers were happy about the drop in production, since this raised coffee prices. By the time this "favourable" loss had turned into incurable loss a few years later, the entire economy was doomed.

In more modern times, the coffee speculators who bought up the coffee warehouses in New York already artificially got around the supply-and-demand theorem, and consumers were obviously cheated.

In 1888, London tried to regulate prices for the first time, with their Coffee and Tea Exchange. Here, coffee lots were auctioned off at the "candle auctions." A candle would be lit, bids were called, and the final bid when the candle flickered out would be the winner. The reliability of this was questionable — but a lot of coffee must have been consumed by the speculators, if only to keep them alert.

Both the New York and London coffee exchanges were relatively efficient up until the Wall Street Crash of 1929. At that time, Brazil — which provided more than 50 per cent of the world's coffee — had to burn more than 25 million bags to get an equitable price.

By the 1940's, it was impossible to make sense of the market. In 1940, coffee sold for seven cents a pound. And while Brazil tried many ways to regulate the price within the country, it failed miserably. Firstly, because of the competition from other countries. Secondly, natural disasters made regulation impossible.

The hardest attempt at regularising came in 1959, with the International Coffee Organisation, which theoretically would regulate quotas from the different coffee-exporting countries. And while that *sounded* plausible it never really worked to anybody's advantage. Anything could interfere with the process: a frost, a dry season, political upheavals, or personal panic.

Brazil did try more ways of keeping prices up than any other country. Today, coffee revenues make up less than 20 per cent of the economy. But when it was over 50 per cent it was obligatory for the Government to help the farmer.

One attempt was "valorization". The Government would purchase coffee from the farmer and withdraw the coffee to create an artificial scarcity until prices were high enough. That too was a failure from the start. It was a major financial operation by the Government, it met with much consumer resistance, and the result was that much coffee was burned, dumped in the ocean or sold cheap to be manufactured as a fertiliser.

The second attempt was banning further plantings after a good year. But a) this could never be enforced; b) when other countries saw what Brazil was doing, they simply planted more, thus lowering the prices. Third was an agreement in 1957 for the South American countries to withhold their coffee. Once again a failure. For by this time, Africa had taken over 20 per cent of the market.

Still, the International Coffee Organisation tried its best in giving quotas for each country. Then came the panic of '75 — the 1975 frost in Brazil which drove coffee prices up so high around the world that the market and quota systems became simply irrelevant. No less than two-thirds of the coffee in Brazil was destroyed by frost.

Today, the coffee market is based on futures and nobody can predict what this will be. The coffee is bought to be delivered at a certain date, a few months or anything up to two years away, with the hope that the price has been correctly estimated.

And how is this done? It is better to work on a system for the roulette wheels of Macau or Las Vegas than to try to figure this market. But some systems in the coffee market are listed below:

a. The Two-Year System

This is the simplest system of all, and has long ago been disproved. It works this way. Every *other* year, coffee trees would be "tired" and wouldn't produce as much as the year before. Someone would bet on trying to buy in the "off-year" when prices would be high to the consumer.

Whatever agricultural promise this had, it has never worked. In theory, the carryover from the "good" crop should take care of the deficit for the following year. But as the entire premise is fallible, the error is compounded over the years, making the margin of error altogether too great, and other countries will always fill up the gap.

b. The Seven-Year Itch

This is theoretically a more reliable way of predicting prices. One takes it for granted that during a good year (i.e., a low yield of coffee and high prices), other planters will switch to coffee, hoping to get in on the good prices. But as it takes from three to five years for coffee trees to bloom, this would take at least five years. During this growing time, the planter is selling crops from trees, investing his profits in clearing more land. But now, as the harvest grows, the market is glutted with coffee. So prices fall, and the planters stop clearing new land. So, as the prices reach their nadir after seven years, already they are ready to go up over the next seven years, until the prices reach their height, and they begin to fall . . .

Does this work? While the seven-year cycle has more credence, it is affected by so many other factors, that no speculator in coffee could possibly take it seriously.

As in roulette, the number five theoretically comes up the same number of times as any other number over an infinite period of time. But in practice, each year — or each number — depends on too much else.

c. The Meteorological System

Meteorologists all have their own theory of "cycles" to predict coffee prices. They have two, three or five-year periods of frost, and usually have the statistics to prove it. But once again, there are too many other factors.

Even more important, since the 1970's, according to most weathermen, "the weather has been so crazy, so screwed up, that nobody can predict anything."

d. The Fundamental Theory

This is one of the two "real" systems, as it takes in virtually every factor dealing with the growing of coffee itself. The Fundamentalist takes into consideration the weather, growing cycles, seven-year-cycles, political upheavals, oil prices, even chemical inventions. He'll look at the economy of the world (if inflation is high, more people might turn to cheaper *robusta* coffee blends, so futures two years hence could be high prices in Brazil where there'll be fewer growers), possible wars and the internal corruption of any given country, (i.e., in Uganda, about half of the coffee is going to be smuggled out, thus confusing the actual statistics of coffee-growing.)

In theory, the Fundamentalists should have the best bets. The problem is, though, that there are so *many* factors that nobody can ever balance out the right

103

Sampling for quality.

emphasis to be given each. Obviously, a frost in Brazil is going to move prices upward sooner or later. But it isn't obvious what a revolution in Timor will do to prices. And ten or 20 cents on one pound has to be multiplied by the 21,000 pounds in a single "lot" of coffee. (Each lot is made up of 250 60-kilogramme bags.)

e. The Technician's Theory

This is the most difficult one of all. The Technician cares nothing at all for growing, most weather fluctuations or mere revolutions. He will look *only* at the charts, and might not know a Blue Mountain coffee bean from a jar of instant. All he knows is that, by following the charts year after year, noting how the graphs run, he can more or less predict what sort of geometrical patterns will be formed by the speculators in the following years.

Is this psychology? Economics? Divination? Or just geometric guesswork?

By reading the commodity reports of the most influential moneyman, one notices a plethora of factors, facts, *past* figures — and grammatically, a glut, a sate, an overabundance of "ifs", "on the other hands", "mays or may nots". Merrill Lynch Pierce Fenner & Smith, for instance, in a May 1979 report on coffee, sums up a very technical graphic report with the words: "What we can say with certainty is that the frost-induced high prices have affected people."

So much for economic expertise!

104

What does all of this have to do with the coffee-grower? On the smallholdings, it usually means that they will be on the lowest edge of the business. In Madagascar, for instance, the coffee-growers on the east coast bring their coffee to the port cities, where the economy is run mainly by Chinese merchants. World prices, exchanges and speculators are in a limbo of their own, and the peasant is offered money which may have nothing to do with reality. In the long run, this can prove to have political repercussions (see the chapter, *Coffee and politics*), but in the short run, the grower cannot be happy.

Both the coffee-speculator and the coffee-grower have largely insoluble problems with their soluble product. But the coffee-importer has a traditional method of insuring against wild price fluctuation: the "coffee hedge." How does this work? To insure against a loss of money, the green-coffee importer may buy in July for delivery to himself during August. He believes that prices will fall, so he will simultaneously sell the same quantity of green coffee, in the form of September delivery, as future contracts on the Coffee Exchange. He has, in effect, agreed to *take* delivery at today's prices and *make* delivery at today's prices. Should the market go down, the coffee is worth less, but

his contract with the Coffee Exchange shows a profit, making up the loss. If the market goes up, then the contract with the Coffee Exchange is worth less, but his own coffee is worth more. And the importer will make his own profit, oblivious to world prices.

Hedging is like paying a premium for an insurance policy against violent and unwanted fluctuations.

And what does this market do for countries like Brazil, Colombia and Tanzania? With the "screwed-up weather", with unstable politics and a fluctuating market, one would hope that Colombia leads the way. In 1980, Colombia spent no less than US$1.2 billion just to diversify and promote other products.

Of course, there's one more theory to take into account. Speculators in coffee have so many sleepless nights thinking about the market that they drink anything *but* coffee. If there are enough speculators in the world, then the number of buyers goes down, and with less demand the prices are lower, and less land is planted and . . .

And let the speculators speculate on *that* conundrum!

"These berries are devil's work! So back to the devil these fruits must go!"

Angry Moslem Imam, roasting the first coffee beans, 850 A.D.

Coffee: The magic roast

Despite the accidental hurling of coffee beans into the fire in the 9th Century, it wasn't until 300 years later that coffee-lovers realised that roasting was such a vital — even magical — means of achieving great coffee flavour.

In the 16th Century, the roasting of coffee was actually prohibited, though this was most likely simply another reason to close down the "seditious" coffee-houses. One *fetwa* (commentary on the Holy Koran) of the time reads "Whatsoever reaches the level of carbonisation, that is, becomes charcoal, is absolutely forbidden."

That was something of an aberration in the history of coffee. But even before roasting became habitual in the 12th Century, the coffee pit was eaten, fermented, turned into either wine or butter. Still, it is universally agreed today that the perfect flavour begins only with the alchemy of perfect roasting. And the word alchemy isn't used lightly here. For contemporary scientists are *still* unable to chemically analyse some of the processes which take place during roasting: it is still a magical roast.

One would imagine that with such a "mundane" process, one would use only mundane words. But when coffee experts discuss roasting, they talk about "the moment of truth", "the mysterious chemistry", "the rush of the aroma" and the head shaman or magician of the whole process, the Roast Master.

Why roasting in the first place? Because *without* roasting, the bean won't give up its flavour. Professional tasters may find something of value in the green bean, but coffee-drinkers are only interested in the roasting process.

What exactly happens in the roasting process? Nobody knows the complete story yet. But one can have an idea by knowing something of the composition of a green coffee bean. The bean is composed of water, oils, protein, caffeine, chlorogenic acid, trigonelline, tannin, caffetannin, caffeic acid, sucrose, starch, acid and vitamins. And all of these are changed during roasting.

Physically the coffee changes in three ways: when the steam, carbon dioxide and carbon monoxide are released, the weight *loss* can be between 14 to 23 per cent. But before miserly coffee-buyers have time to regret this, remember that the internal pressure of the gas *expands* the volume of the bean by 30 to 100 per cent!

106

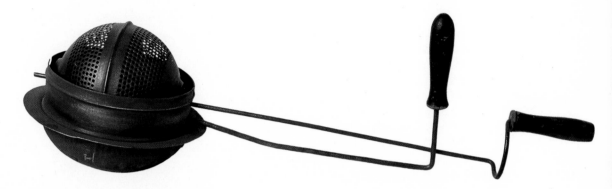

Home coffee-roaster from the 19th Century.

The third physical aspect of change is the colour. Depending upon the length of roasting, the bean will change from green to brown, all of this controlled by the Roast Master. Depending upon its later use, the bean can go from green to light brown to deep rich brown to near-black. Chemically, this is due to the sucrose caramelising on the outside.

The most important aspect is the taste and aroma. And nobody can explain this thoroughly.

When the aromatic hydrocarbons are roasted, they turn to a kind of taste-stimulating acid, which, with the caffeine (which doesn't change), produces the pleasant bitter taste. Already, a mystery emerges here. For, as the acids are created, they are also destroyed. Because of the time difference, it would seem that a light-roasted coffee would have the most acid and, in theory, would have the most flavour. But

it is not so. For, along with the acids, there are other flavour-inducing substances. Tannin and caffeine also provide an astringency and pleasant taste. So does the trigonelline — though nobody is yet certain what this adds.

Coffee-roaster circa 1900.

The aroma is equally important — and equally mysterious. No less than seventy different chemical compounds have been traced which give off that seductive aroma. But nobody is yet certain *exactly* what happens. All that the Roast Master knows for certain is that, when the oils are released in the roasting, when (to simplify it to one basic) the carbon dioxide is produced with the chemicals, then the aroma comes out, and the Roast Master has found the "moment of truth", or the "volatisation" of the bean. At this point, the roast should be done and ready for packing after cooling.

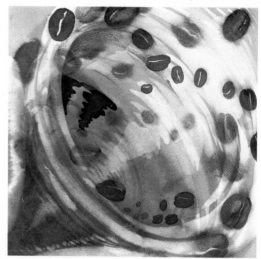

Top: Melitta's modern hot-air roasting process.

Left: Early 20th Century coffee-roaster.

If the chemistry is complicated, the mechanics are . . . well, mechanical. For commercial uses, there are only two basic ways of roasting the bean, and both resemble a kind of spin-dryer.

In the oldest method, coffee in a metal cylinder is roasted above a source of heat: charcoal, gas or electricity, with the temperatures raised to about 220-230 degrees C. This is called singeing. The more common method is to put the beans in a cylinder and blow hot air onto them, gradually raising the heat until the beans are done.

The normal time, depending on what sort of roast is needed, can be between 7 to 18 minutes. And the beans are so sensitive that nobody can leave them to cool on

108

their own. Once they reach the optimum "moment of truth", the beans must be taken out and laid on a cool substance (like marble), and/or sprayed with cool water. Otherwise, they could continue to bake by themselves.

What are the different kinds of roasts? Basically there are only four:
a. *Light roast* This is a delicate roast, and the coffee is good for breakfast, blending excellently with milk and sugar.
b. *Medium roast* A stronger coffee, close to the way the French like their coffee.
c. *Dark roast* Spanish and Cuban coffee is roasted like this. It does give a "darker" smokier flavour.
d. *Double/Continental/Espresso* As the name says, almost black, ready to make espresso or Turkish-type coffee.

Does coffee have to be roasted by a Roast Master with a huge cylinder? Not necessarily. It does make things easy and practical. But for those who take their coffee ritual seriously, one can roast green beans right on the kitchen stove — with much practice and probably very little success at first.

One should use a very heavy frying pan. One puts a single layer of beans in the pan, roasting them on a medium slow fire, then a quick high heat towards the end. The pan must be shaken continuously, and the beans must be turned constantly to assure an even roast. The fire must be stopped just *before* the optimum colour needed.

Or one can use a roasting tin in the oven. The tin should be placed in a pretty hot oven for 20 to 40 minutes, depending on whether light or dark roast is needed.

The advantages are not all that great. But one might have some sense of satisfaction and one might imitate the Ethiopians, who throw the most aromatic spices in with the beans just at the end of roasting. Cloves, cinnamon, nutmeg, fennel, cardamom (my own favourite) and ginger. These are ground up with the beans.

In Europe, the French sometimes add roast sugar, and the Italians add a little butter with sugar to the beans.

The most important part is to cool the beans immediately — and then seal them in an air-tight glass container. Remember that the beans may start losing their flavour just as soon as they are roasted. But this can be slowed down considerably with the right kind of container.

And when ready for brewing, one takes the beans out for the equally important grinding process.

Melitta's experienced coffee samplers.

Coffee: The ground's the limit

Coffee-grinding has a rather unnecessary mystique. No less a personage than Antoine Brillat-Savarin conducted what must have been a fearfully tiresome experiment. He took some Mocha coffee beans and studiously pounded them with mortar and pestle, then took an equal amount and ground them down between two wheels. And then he got his friends to do the same thing, and they sampled the beans and decided that the wheel was better than the pestle.

Novelist Saul Bellow went into similar ecstasies in *Mr. Sammler's Planet*, in which Mr. Sammler explained the joy of grinding coffee in a square box. By doing this he achieved "Acknowledgement of social descent. Historical ruin. Transformation of society."

Whatever the poetic notion, there is a general impression that only by grinding coffee immediately before brewing will the flavour be preserved. This is not exactly true. If one grinds coffee and leaves it lying out in the open air for a few hours, the coffee will certainly start to lose its flavour.

But if the coffee beans are ground just before the coffee is brewed, there is still no guarantee of when the beans were *roasted*; therefore, much of the coffee flavour could already have been lost. (In Europe, for instance, beans on the market shelves more than eight days are usually removed and sold for industrial uses, as they are believed to be already lacking in flavour).

On the other hand, companies such as Melitta take only freshly roasted beans, which are then finely cut (not ground), and packaged in air-tight packages within 45 minutes of being processed, so virtually no flavour is lost, even weeks after being put on the shelves. In all but the most modern packaging, moisture and oxygen blend in with the oils released by grinding to change the flavour. But in air-tight packs, there is only the most fractional change of aroma or flavour.

Some curious coffee-drinkers have queried why unground coffee beans cannot simply be packaged in vacuum packs and placed on market shelves. The answer makes good chemical sense. Once coffee is roasted, most of the gases are released to the air. But even after cooling, the coffee bean exudes more gases into the air. So obviously by immediately packaging in a vacuum-pack, one might risk an explosion of coffee beans.

112

Melitta's modern packaging plant for ground coffee in vacuum packs.

Melitta has helped to develop a "balloon pack" which avoids these problems for unground beans, but vacuum-packs are out of the question.

So what motivation is there for home-grinding at all? Saul Bellow claims that grinding (especially hand-grinding) gives one a sense of history, of older, perhaps more atavistic cultures existing even within our own "modern" culture.

Another motivation is more aromatic than romantic. When one grinds one's own coffee, there is a single particularly magical moment during the grinding process when the oils of the bean are released, and the aroma comes drifting up through the grinder.

That aroma has nothing to do with caffeine or taste or looks. It is pure smell: half-ambrosial, half-pungently bitter. And to a coffee-lover, no more seductive aroma exists.

When it comes to grinding of coffee, only two points of information are needed. A. What kind of grinder should be used? B. How fine should the coffee be ground? Now sit down with your coffee and learn the answers.

A. Kinds of grinders

There are only three kinds of grinders. The virtues and liabilities are discussed below.

1. Mortar and pestle
This is the oldest method of grinding coffee (and most other grains, for that matter). The mortar is a stone bowl, the pestle is a stone instrument for grinding up the coffee in the mortar. The latter was immortalised when Danny Kaye sang "The pellet with the poison's in the vessel with the pestle, the chalice from the palace has the brew that is true."

Virtues: Mortar and pestle builds strong muscles. It is aesthetically beautiful, and a novelty. It's a beautiful tool. One feels a sense of history (and it is still used by some Arabs today).

Liabilities: Impossible to get uniform grind. Time-consuming. Impossible to get the really fine grind needed for special blends. Note: Those who really want to

Antique coffee-grinders, year and country unknown.

try mortar and pestle should make a trip to Thailand. A few miles from Pattaya Beach is the tiny village of Angsila-on-the-Sea where the finest stone mortars and pestles are made. They can be purchased along the main road near Cholburi, but the enjoyment of watching them being made is worth the few miles' journey.

2. Manual coffee-grinding

The Turks were the ones who invented the two wheels which revolve around each other grinding grains. Movies like *Spartacus* and *Ben Hur*, usually show scenes of slaves pushing the millstones around and around to grind the grain. This is the same theory as employed in coffee-grinding.

The stones are now corrugated plates. One is stationary, the other is rotated, and the coffee is ground.

Virtues: The variety of grinders. One can get little boxes for hand-grinding in which coffee seeds are placed on top to be ground, and

Antique brass coffee-grinders found in Vienna, year and country unknown.

115

emerge at the bottom. One can buy grinders which can be attached to the wall. The Turks used to give their soldiers absolutely marvellous three-tiered grinders; the top for keeping the coffee, the middle for grinding, the bottom for lighting a fire under water and boiling the coffee. Grinders can consist of squat metal drums, baroque brass devices, or beautiful wooden boxes. Supermarkets have big grinders with knobs, selection dials for exact amounts of coffee. Another advantage is that it is possible, by regulating the wheels, to get the most consistent grinding.

Liabilities: Too much muscle-work. One cannot get the *finest* ground. It's old-fashioned. (Which may not be such a disadvantage for the coffee ritualist.)

3. The electric grinder

Let's face it, this is the 20th Century. And the electric grinder, even if it works on the same principle as the Turkish mill-stones, is the way to grind coffee. It is cheap, practical and can achieve the same result in a more convenient manner. The disadvantages are very minor indeed.

The household type, small electric grinder, consists of a heavy-duty plastic cylinder with an electric motor. The top is a plastic cap which snaps on. Inside are two millstones. One pours in the coffee

Electric coffee-mill.

beans, presses the button, and within five to ten seconds, the grinds are ready.

Virtues: Easy to operate and cheap. The rush of the aroma is wonderful. The machine is easy to clean and it takes just a few inches of the shelf space.

Disadvantages: No home grinder can grind as evenly and as well as the industrial grinder used by a company like Melitta, which offers a range of fresh pre-ground coffee. By using an electric grinder one cannot control the degree of grinding the coffee to suit different coffee preparation equipment.

The close substitute of the electric grinder is the electric mill with blades on top. The electric mill grinds coffee by cutting and bombarding coffee beans with the blades at a high speed. This will heat up the coffee and the strong outflow of aroma simpy means that the beans are overheated and re-roasted again.

B. Grades of grinding

There are only four basic kinds of grinds — but they are extremely important for the kind of coffee you want.

1. Coarse:
This is used only for coffee-making in a jug, where the coffee is steeped, in a percolator or boiling the grounds directly. It isn't very economic as it takes the longest brewing time for the water to extract the oils, and the extraction is weak at best. On the other hand, less of the aroma disappears with the grinding, and it can be preserved for the cup. When storing medium-grind coffee, the aroma evaporates quicker, because of the ventilation.

2. Medium:
This comes out like granulated sugar. The drip pot makes fine coffee, and it is used for the vacuum method of coffee-making.

3. Filter:
Certainly the most common grind. About eight seconds in the electric grinder should do it. Melitta coffee is best with Very Fine, as it slows down the flow of water. Espresso coffee is also better. Anything finer than this would actually clog the filter.

4. Pulverised:
This is used for Turkish coffees, and for short brewing times. Thai coffee is also made this way. So much oil is extracted so quickly that it can have a rather bitter taste. But laced with sugar the way the Turks like it, pulverised coffee is perfect.

There is a *very* coarse grind - but this is used only for brewing large quantities of coffee for industrial purposes, when time is not of great importance.

It must be noted that home-grinding is enjoying a renaissance at the moment, although most buyers, especially in Asia, prefer to have their coffees pre-ground and ready in tins or packages. One can sympathise with this time-saving process, especially with scientific breakthroughs in packaging.

But for coffee-snobs and romantics of any age, nothing can beat the aroma of coffee which has been ground just before brewing.

Tasting and blending

British wit Clement Freud speaks despairingly of coffee-snobs as being more insufferable than wine-snobs. Be that as it may, Freud is right in comparing the two, except for one aspect of tasting. Virtually every gourmet considers himself *something* of an expert in wine-tasting — but rare indeed is the coffee-lover who can spot even the country or countries from which his coffee comes.

True coffee-tasting ability, in fact, is so rare that it is said the entire United States coffee market is determined by less than *40* tasters! This is probably true, since the New York Coffee and Sugar Exchange, which controls the market, employs only 31 tasters for all the coffee imported into the country. But these are tasters who are *tasters*! Each morning they come to their office at 79 Pine Street and sit around a table which has nothing but pans of green and roasted drip-ground beans. On the side is a three-foot high spittoon known as a "garboon". (The garboon's etymology is particularly obscure, as the only other definition of the word is for an extremely rare type of bassoon.) What they go through each morning and afternoon is not a ritual or a ceremony: it is a highly scientific, fairly objective taste and smell and look at coffee. And their knowledge and memory must be extraordinary — for, when they refer to "coffee-green", they aren't speaking of unroasted beans, they're speaking of money in the coffee futures markets!

Basically, tasters in America and Europe — whether the New York Exchange for *arabica* beans, the London Exchange for *robusta*, master-tasters for Melitta in Germany, or for the rare coffee speciality shops around the world — have the same system. So perfect is this system that it has rarely changed over 250 years. And variations in different countries are minor.

The following are the steps in professional coffee-tasting.

a. Presentation
Coffee is laid out in two pans, green and roasted. By each taster's place is a clean white cup to hold around six ounces, a silver teaspoon, a cup of water for washing the spoon between tastings, a garboon for spitting, and a kettle of boiling water.

b. The sight test
The green beans are examined thoroughly, and imperfections noted. No coffee sample is perfect, and one expects to find "bad" beans. But if too many are discovered, the entire bag from

118

which the sample was taken may go back to the sample envelopes or may be sold for industrial uses.

Imperfections may include twigs, ''parchment'' beans with the skin left on, or ''pod'' beans with two

Herr Obrock, Melitta's master coffee blender.

seeds in the bean. Broken beans, those with too many variations in colour, and unripe beans are all rejected.

c. The aroma test
This is also called the "wet smell" or the "crust test." Boiling water is poured in the china cup which contains two level tablespoons of fresh and finely drip-ground coffee. The grounds will form a crust on top of the water. The taster almost literally sticks his nose into the crust to inhale the first great draughts of aroma. He breaks the crust and sniffs again. Then he spoons up some of the grounds from the bottom after breaking the crust and sniffs a third time.

d. The taste test
After the crust is broken, most of the grounds should be settling in the bottom. Whatever is left on top should be spooned out and thrown into the garboon. But once the water has cooled a *little* bit, the taster takes a spoonful of the coffee to his mouth. He doesn't suck it in delicately like wine — but violently, noisily inhales it into the back of his mouth, even spraying his palate. There are two reasons for this inhalation. First, by spraying it in, he aerates the coffee, maximising the flavour. Second, by spraying the *back* of his mouth, he is minimising the salivation, which could dilute the taste.

e. The body-and-acidity test
He doesn't swallow the coffee, but instead rolls the coffee in the mouth. With practice, he can practically chew the coffee. (And neophytes to tasting obviously *will* be chewing the awful grounds in the cup.)

Finally, he spits the coffee out in the garboon and goes onto the next test after a little sip of water or some bread.

Is all of this testing absolutely necessary? One might well ask whether a concert violinist should tune up before a performance. The slightest flatness of a note might not strike the occasional listener — but multiplied many times by an orchestra, the music will sound very dissonant indeed. A single cup of bad coffee might not be too striking. But when dealing with 60-kilogramme bags, every single bag from a different plantation or country or altitude where each section of each plantation has its own distinct differences, the extraordinary memory and sensitivity of the taster is essential. Which is why the taster has such a variety of regal names (the "liquorer", the "cupper"), and why he is considered the aristocrat of the industry.

What exactly is the taster looking for in coffee? This is where the special coffee vocabulary comes in, through four separate categories.

1. The acid test

Acidity is a bad word in wine, but hardly bad in coffee. *Acid* is the tartness, the tang, the snap which one feels in the back of the mouth. Much acidity, as in Ethiopian Mocha coffee, is called *winey* taste. Coffee from India or Venezuela, may be *sweet* or *mellow*. Brazilian coffees are prized very much for their "right" amount of *acid*, which is called *richness*.

2. Body

No coffee is "heavier" than another. But many somehow feel heavier in the mouth. Coffee from Indonesia, especially Sumatra, is very heavy and has much *body*. Ethiopian Mocha has the least body. The best Brazilian is in the middle. With light-bodied coffees, the flavour is so delicate that one should never add milk.

3. Aroma

This is a combination of acidity and flavour. Acidy coffee smells *acidy*, richly-flavoured coffees smell *richly-flavoured*. Some coffees are more fragrant than others. For the most aroma, Jamaican Blue Mountain, Sumatran and Colombian are ideal.

4. Flavour

Flavour can be described endlessly. Flavour, in the last resort, is what coffee is all about. Some drinkers enjoy a very *distinctive* flavour, as in *chocolatey* Ethiopian. Sumatran has a *rich* flavour. Brazilian coffee is sometimes preferred because it has no really distinctive flavour but it *blends* in perfectly. Wild or *mellow* coffees have little acidity or tang but do have much body. On the other end of the scale are *harsh* coffees. These are bitter and sharp and unpleasant, but sometimes a bit of *harsh* coffee in a *bland* blend brings out certain flavour characteristics.

Coffee epithets are in a class of their own. *Hidey, sour, muddy, grassy, barnyard fermented.* These terms are used for the lowest grades of coffee.

Now comes the unanswerable question: What is the Perfect Blend of coffee?

This is like asking for the Perfect Performance of *Othello*, or the Perfect Sunset or the Perfect Stereo System. It has no answer. Personal taste counts for everything. Taste and the occasion.

Some like their black morning coffee heavily acidic, lightbodied, mellow tasting. Others like a brisk light coffee with much body. Others want an all-round coffee. Others like a certain country's — though it is rare to have an unblended coffee.

Here, though, are a few hints on coffee combinations:

1. Pergaminos.
2. Maragogype.
3. Central America, washed.
4. Kenya, washed.
5. Perlcoffees.
6. Brazil, unwashed.
7. Robusta.

For a middle-of-the-road combination of flavour, strength and aroma, one can combine the best beans of Colombia, Java and Brazil. A stronger coffee with a rich bouquet would include Colombia. With Hawaiian Kona, Brazil and Java coffee, you might have the ultimate coffee which is rich, strong with an outstanding flavour.

On a general basis, the Central American coffees have a lot of snap and acidity. Tanzania and Sumatra add body and richness. Venezuelan coffee adds sweetness. And those who want much sweetness should try an aged coffee, or, if possible, an Indian blend. Flavour and aroma which is distinctive comes with Jamaican Blue Mountain, with Indonesian and Colombian coffee. And the rich, winey, almost chocolatey flavour comes with Ethiopian Mocha, with Kenya coffee or, if you should be so lucky, Arabian Mocha.

Melitta blends change from country to country. But their four blends sold in Asia give a good idea of the spectrum of coffee tastes. The Blue Mountain Blend has Jamaican Blue Mountain beans with the finest *arabica* beans, for a mild to medium-bodied aromatic coffee. Melitta Mocha is a more full-bodied blend of *arabica* beans, dark roasted, with a smooth background and a subtle strength.

Melitta knows Germany well, so their German Premium Blend is for those from northern Europe (and lovers of North European coffee) who want a mild aromatic coffee. The American Extra blend is made almost entirely with South American beans which have a smooth body and a nutty flavour.

When it comes down to it, though, that great philosopher — and great coffee-drinker — Friedrich Nietzsche has the last word. "All of life," he wrote "is a dispute over taste and of tasting."

Melitta's worldwide range of coffee.

123

The instant solution

That very funny and erudite British wit-gourmet Clement Freud once told a radio audience how to serve the most appreciated coffee at a dinner party.

First, he said, buy green beans in the afternoon. Before the dinner, show them to your guests, and modestly excuse yourself to put the beans in the oven to roast. Leave the oven door open during dinner so the aroma spreads through the dining room. After the final course, when the guests are oohing and ahhing and being seduced by the aroma, you secretly open a jar of instant coffee (the *best* instant coffee), and serve *this* up to the admiration of the guests. Freud is certain that they'll never know the difference!

True coffee-lovers disapprove of this prostitution of the coffee bean. But statistics show that more than a quarter of all coffee consumed is the soluble variety known world-wide as "instant." Significantly, in under-developed coffee markets, the ratio of instant to fresh is 9:1. In developed markets (in other words, those who know their coffee), it's 1:9. Coffee lovers insist that a drink cannot be called "coffee" after the flavour, aroma and 50 per cent of the weight has been extracted.

On the other hand, instant coffee *is* cheap and it *is* convenient. The invention of soluble coffee began with a discovery in 1906 by an English chemist living in Guatemala. He noticed the powdery deposits which collected on the spout of his coffee pot, and set about producing them on a large scale. Three years later, he was marketing his Red E coffee, and other patented brands quickly followed.

The demand for instant coffee was stimulated by the needs of soldiers in the two world wars, and the periodic shortage of ground coffee. The invention was also welcomed by Brazil as a means of selling its huge surplus between the wars.

While ground coffee has its mystery and romance, instant coffee is all business. The oldest method of processing is known as spray drying. It begins with a large number of bags of undistinguished *robusta* and *liberica* coffee being blended and roasted very dark. (No quality coffee is used, as it would be too expensive, and the subtle flavour would be lost.) The roast is ground and put into a building-size percolator, and brewed under very high pressures and temperatures. This causes the cellulose in the coffee to be converted into soluble

carbohydrates, creating bulk —
while taking away most of the
flavour.

This brew is then spread into a
tall drying chamber in which hot
air is circulated. When the coffee
reaches the bottom of the
chamber, all the water has
evaporated, and the grains of
powder are left. This is "instant"
coffee.

What about the coffee aroma? The
coffee manufacturers try to
simulate the aroma of real coffee
by adding coffee oil to the
finished product. This creates an
aroma when the jar is first
opened. But it doesn't add
anything to the real flavour. And
the coffee powder tends to turn
rancid after the jar has been left
standing.

The newest process is called
"freeze-drying", and the coffee
does look and taste better. Instead
of subjecting the coffee to steam
— a steam which *over*-extracts the
flavour — the percolated coffee is
cooled to a slushy consistency,
frozen solid and broken into
granules. It is then placed in a
vacuum chamber, where the air
pressure is lowered as the
temperature is raised. The water
is drawn off and the solid
granules remain. More of the
flavour is retained than in the
older method, but at least 31
per cent of the coffee is no more
than carbohydrate bulk.

The perfect cup of coffee

Of course there is no perfect cup of coffee — which means that there is no "dull" cup of coffee. Coffee is not simply a taste. If so, one could prepare the taste at any time for any occasion. Rather, coffee is a delicate balance between taste, aroma, body, look and feel. This is only the beginning. Further permutations, involving cream, sugar, cardamom, ginger, vanilla, rum, or whiskey, add wider dimensions. And even if one has the right permutations, there is no way to guarantee that the perfect blend of coffee from one year will be equally perfect the next year. Like wine, coffee can change even on the same plantation from one year to the next. Coffee-blenders may cheapen blends for price reasons, or because of a new roasting problem. Add to this the variety of brewing machines, the quality of the water, even that all-important psychological factor of the serving apparatus, or the occasion (A coffee mug on the morning of a hangover is universes away from coffee from a silver pot after a gourmet meal, even if the blend is exactly the same.)

Yet with all these factors, there *are* certain rules which can at least prepare the groundwork for interesting cups of coffee.

Certain rules are inflexible. One is cleanliness. The *New York Times* cooking guru, Craig Claiborne, makes this a cardinal rule. "The most important thing in coffee-making," he writes in *Kitchen Primer*, "is the cleanliness of the pot. It should be scrubbed well after each use and washed with soap and water . . . The grinds may in almost all circumstances be put down the drain of the kitchen sink."

The second rule is the water. Soft water means an astringency, a sourness in the taste. Medium hard, straight from the tap, is best. It should be unboiled, as the chemical components of the water must blend in with the chemical components of the coffee grounds.

Third, one must harmonise the type of ground with the right brewing machinery. If one were to make espresso with coarse ground, the result would simply be a weak coffee. For a percolator, though, coarse or middle fine ground is best. Very fine ground is perfect for the coffee filter method like Melitta. For espresso or the Turkish *ibrik* coffee method, very fine pulverised coffee is essential.

And when one brews the coffee, timing is of vital importance. The optimum amount of soluble coffee

materials had been 19 percent of the coffee weight. More than that had resulted in bitterness, less meant very weak coffee. But with the Melitta system, up to 25 per cent can be extracted, so fewer coffee grounds are necessary.

It is a mistaken notion to believe that one is "cooking" the coffee, and that one can control the taste by percolating or boiling the coffee longer than necessary. The *real* cooking is done when the coffee beans are roasted. So one must pay attention to *extracting the maximum flavour* from the beans, not changing the flavour.

Left: Antique silver coffee-pot, year and origin unknown.

Below: Antique coffee-pot, Germanisches Museum Nuremberg.

With fine grind, water circulates through more coffee "area", so one to two minutes per cup is best. Medium drip grind is three to four minutes, and the coarse grind, where the water runs through the grind area more slowly, can take up to six minutes.

One should *never* either boil the coffee or let boiling water touch the coffee. If the water is boiling, it will extract too many bitter and unpleasant elements. Rather, be certain that the water is just *below* boiling. Coffee should be consumed as quickly as possible after brewing in order to experience the aroma with the flavour.

Keeping coffee hot is not difficult. Coffee pots — everything from romantic Arab pots with their S-shaped spouts to English silver and porcelain pots — are all practical.

The coffee cup is equally important. For double-strength Italian espresso or Arabic *ibrik*, demitasse cups are ideal for soaking in the perfume. Cappuccino, Mocha and other "speciality" coffees have their own specialty mugs, but these aren't necessary in the home. On the other hand,

Antique brass coffee-pots.

Antique brass coffee-pot with stove.

Antique coffee cup origin unknown.

for ordinary coffees, good heavy
ceramic mugs or cups (preferably
warmed first in hot water) are
ideal. Unless one prefers either
delicate china, or, as the Germans
and Scandinavians do, porcelain
cups.

The art of coffee-cups is a very
complex one, and no less a
commentator than that tea-lover,

Samuel Johnson, acknowledged
coffee's mastery. When Boswell
inquired as to whether beauty
was independent of utility, Dr.
Johnson replied with the coffee-
cup. Picking it up, he pointed to
the painting on the cup, which,
he said, was "of no real use. As
the cup would be equally useful if
plain. Yet the painting was
beautiful."

Shakespeare and coffee.

It is not generally known, but William Shakespeare wrote *Hamlet* originally not as a tragedy about the Prince of Denmark but as a guide to eating healthy breakfasts for an Elizabethan version of *Sesame Street*. (The original title of the drama was *Hamlet And Egglets*.)

And the famous Players' Scene was composed originally with Hamlet instructing not a group of travelling actors but a group of *coffee*-makers! Believe it or not, all the information given by Hamlet to these brewers will stand up today, so this scene should be read, memorised and the instructions followed, in order to make the perfect cup of coffee.

Hamlet: The Brewers' Scene

Enter HAMLET with POLONIUS and four or five BREWERS

Hamlet: Welcome, good brewers, welcome all. What hast thou?

Polonius: Aye, what hast thou for my master Hamlet?

First brewer: We have all manner coffee for thee, my liege.

Polonius (Aside): Coffee? That dost bode well in this troubled reign: For tis said that coffee doth stimulate the brain.

(To Hamlet): I think, m'lord, that a single coffee cup, With the warmth of thy benificence And the sweetness of my Ophelia's breast Would be most festive an addition In this troubled land.

Hamlet (Aside): It would be so indeed, If the milk of *thy* Ophelia's breast Were in *my* coffee cup to rest.

(To Polonius): Enough from thee and me, Polonius. Speak, my percolating friends and say What sorts of coffee thou hast brought today. Dost include mild Santos from Brazil? Chocolatey Mocha from the land of Araby? Dost thou have sweet grounds from the Indies East? And delicate Blue Mountain from the Indies West?

Second brewer: Aye, dost include better and the best.

Polonius (Aside): More? This coffee will, methinks, ignite
Amongst the sleepiest folk a wakening delight.
Hamlet: Hush, thou, old Polonius, let the brewers speak
About their perfect cup of coffee so unique.
Third brewer: Perfection, m'lord, is found not in our coffee
Or e'en in the stars, but in ourselves,
In our own preference for taste and touch and smell.
Fourth brewer: Aye, for only those in darkest ignorance believe
That one man's perfect roast should be suitable to all.
Hamlet: That is true. What is mud to one,
To th'other will enthrall.
First brewer: One begins, m'lord, with the ground itself,
That it should suit the length of brewing time.
Second brewer: Fine grind, though which water runs swiftly through,
Should be brewed for minutes three or two;
Medium drip grind, minutes four to six;
And regular or coarse grind, six to eight.
Polonius: Aye, but what about strength? Please formulate.
I prefer *my* coffee heavy with body,
Whilst Ophelia requires more delicate a brew.
First brewer: Then, my liege, the ratio must remain true.
'Tis usual for level tablespoons two
To fill up six ounces of water,
But for thy stronger brew,
The same level tablespoons two,
One *half* cup water only thou fillst up.
Polonius: That seemeth the wisest way to sup
From the usual eight-ounce cup.
But what about the water itself?
Are there special rules?
Should we boil the water first?
First brewer: Not unless thou hast perverted thirst.
Third brewer: Water is as important as ground, m'lord.
For the water must be cold and fresh,
And never, never boiled beforetimes.
First brewer: And make certain that the water be as soft as possible
So as to omit all bitterness.
Polonius: And what temperature, sirrah, shalt the water be?
First brewer: When beginning, water must be cold,
But when it boils, be certain it toucheth not
The grounds as it boils, but just below that point,
Lest too much be extracted from the coffee.
Second brewer: Remember never to brew coffee in haste,
So as to bring together body, aroma and taste.

Polonius: Enough now!
    Thou hast excited our sense
    to no end.
Hamlet: Nay, Polonius, thou art
    very wrong:
    For these brewers excite our
    senses
    To the glorious and tasteful
    end.
    I commend thee all.
Third brewer: Then instruct us,
    m'lord in our own art.
Hamlet: Coffee, my friends is
    partly art, but mostly craft.
    First, thou must brew the
    coffee
    So it sits trippingly on
    the tongue.
First brewer: 'Tis good advice indeed.
Hamlet: Be not too tame in thy
    coffee,
    But let your discretion
    be your tutor.
    Brew it always at full
    strength, observing
    That thou preparest not in
    cheap metal,
    But in steel or tinned copper
    or glass jug,
    And that this jug be ever
    washed after use:
    For e'en the best coffee
    tasteth rancid and not new
    If polluted with oily residue.
    Let taste be a mirror of the
    taster.
    For with the right grind and
    brewing time,
    The perfect cup can be the cup
    sublime.
    Give strong black coffee in
    the morning,
    Light and stimulating

after heavy meals.
    Let the romance of the desert
    be in thy home
    With but a dash of ginger or
    seed of cardamom.
    Or let the taste jump out with
    salt.
    Nor should'st forget cream or
    brown sugar,
    Which complements, nay
    addeth that to coffee
    Which imagination addeth
    not, in sum.
    At times, tis heaven, too, to
    pour brandy or e'en rum:
    Alcohol is oft employed to
    round off coffee's taste,
    For spirits and coffee have,
    like lovers, oft embraced.
    (Exeunt HAMLET)
First brewer: Whither goeth this
    coffee expert now?
Polonius: Hamlet hath become so
    seduced by his own teaching
    That he to the fire goeth to
    practice what he's preaching.
Second brewer: Aye, and look: for
    he bringeth forth his coffee.
Polonius: Now cracks a noble bean.
    May perfect taste suit thy
    perfect brew,
    Sweet prince: at first a sip,
    and then adieu.

Exeunt

    *   *   *

What a shame that this scene, certainly an improvement on the later Players' Scene, is not performed these days.

Making it: The final step

Writer Kenneth Davids has one way of looking at the brewing of coffee: "No matter what they're called," he writes in *The Coffee Book*, "all ways of brewing coffee are basically the same: you soak the ground coffee in the water until the water tastes good, and then you drink it. Nobody . . . has figured out a different way to make coffee."

Perhaps he's right. But walk into any department store in Japan, Sydney, London, New York and all points east and west and see the remarkable equipment used just to "soak the coffee in water." The most remarkable machines are available here, and the naive (if enthusiastic) coffee-maker may easily get confused between French drip pots, Etruscan, Biggins, syphons, Konas, English boil pots, filters, stills, vacuums and of course filter pots.

Fortunately, one may divide coffee-making into two basic categories.
a) Decoction (boiling)
b) Infusion (filtering)

Except for making Turkish coffee, one need not worry too much about decoction. Decoction means simply that one boils a substance (in this case ground coffee) until the flavour is extracted. Decoction was the earliest way of making coffee and is still used throughout the Middle East. Romantics who like to conjure up images of Old Araby, and those who love very strong coffee, prepare the beverage with a small copper pot which has a long handle and narrow neck, the Turkish *ibrik*. (Or, the Arabic *kanaka* or Greek *briki*.) The finest grind is used, and coffee-making is more a ritual than a simple boiling.

For each demitasse to be made, three ounces of water are warmed in the *ibrik*. Then, a tablespoon overflowing with coffee is poured on top, together with sugar, and any spices desired, such as cardamom. When the water boils, you move the pan off the fire for a few moments, return it to the boil again, remove it, and then bring to a third boil.

The result is a foamy pungent brew with a good Arabian bite. Coffee speciality shops in Europe and America sell *ibriks* of different sizes and even in Hong Kong and Tokyo such has been the interest in coffee that *ibriks* are readily available.

When serving the coffee, one should say to each person "Semm", or "Say the name of God", to which the guest replies "Bismillah" or "To God".

Traditionally, a plate of dates should be served with the coffee. Not simply for geographical affinities, but because dates, dipped in a little butter, have a special taste affinity with coffee.

The only other decoction method is the jug method, used in 18th Century England and France, and in the traditional cowboy films. The latter is called hobo coffee. Also known as the open-pot method, it is a simple and hardly satisfactory way of making coffee. But it's certainly the easiest. One brings water in a saucepan to a boil. One adds the right amount of coffee (a regular grind, never very fine or pulverised). Stir. Turn off the heat and cover, letting it steep (stand) for five minutes. Pour out either through a filter or very carefully.

The newest trendy device is available all through Asia in a seemingly "sophisticated" plunger, which looks wonderful but doesn't have any other advantage. One steeps the coffee grounds and water in a very elegant jar under a plunger with a very fine filter screen. Then the plunger is pressed down, and the grounds are filtered out. The coffee taste is not improved, the pot must be washed extremely carefully to get rid of the oily residue, the water is usually lukewarm . . . but it looks very impressive.

One other method is that of coffee concentrate. This was originally used by the Incas of Peru (see under *The world of coffeecups*), but the Dutch in the East Indies used the same method in storing coffee. It simply means steeping in cold water for a long time and keeping the concentrate for a later use.

Infusion is the most common method of making coffee. Essentially, infusion means extracting coffee flavour at a temperature just *below* boiling, and with a filter or cloth so that the coffee beans themselves never touch the water. This way, no coffee grounds ever reach the water (only the "body", the flavour and the aroma). There is little bitterness. Of the hundreds of variations, the following show the most important classes.

a. The South American Bag

This is one of the oldest methods, and certainly the simplest. South Americans truly love their coffee, and they put the dark-roasted, finely-ground coffee into a cloth bag known as a *coador* (literally, a sieve), and boiling water is poured through the bag into a pot. This method produces coffee with a strong body, but it can be rather messy, and it necessitates constant laundering of the bag.

In Asia, the Thais and Laotians make coffee basically the same way.

b. The Drip Pot

Basic, old, and satisfactory is the drip pot, invented at the end of the 18th Century by a Frenchman, and popularised by an American (who became a Count of the Holy Roman Empire)! This pot consists of two compartments, an upper and lower, divided by a metal or ceramic filter.

The coffee is placed in the upper compartment, and hot water is poured over it. If done *slowly* and *carefully* enough, the brewed coffee will drip slowly down into the bottom compartment.

While rarely seen today, the Italians have a variation of this in the so-called "Neapolitan Pot", or "Flip Pot." This consists of a metal pot with the same two containers separated by a filter. This is placed on the heat with the spouted part, upside-down, on top. When the water boils (as indicated by steam hissing from a special pinhole), the pot is flipped over, and the coffee pours into the serving container.

Coffee-maker with ceramic top.

18th Century tin coffee-maker.

136

c. The Vacuum System (Syphon)

The most complete, complex, elaborate and first filtration system was invented in 1840 by Robert Napier, a Scottish engineer. The Napier Vacuum coffee-maker consisted of a glass globe containing the water, and a glass bowl with the coffee. Between them was a tight-fitting filter of cloth or metal.

The coffee was heated and rose up as steam through the filter into the coffee. Then the machine was moved from the heat. And, as a vacuum had been formed in the globe, the brewed coffee was drawn *into* it through the filter.

The coffee was good — and it provided aesthetic pleasure. But it was too complicated, and the glass bowls too fragile for common use. Today, though, many fine hotels use a variation of this in the Cona or Silex coffee-makers. This makes coffee with a spirit lamp or an electric heater, and it makes for a beautiful sight — as well as giving a fairly modern look at an old process.

Right: Syphon coffee-maker, very popular in Japan.

Left: 19th Century pewter coffee-container heated with spirit lamp.

d. The Percolator

The original percolator was actually like the drip pot described above. The next step was the "Pumping Percolator", also developed in France in 1827. This was designed to heat the water and brew the coffee in one operation, by *pumping* the hot water through the grounds. Except for the electric percolator — supposedly used to regulate the heat of the water automatically — this is exactly what is used today.

Modern electric percolator.

The percolator provides an easy and convenient way of brewing coffee, but one must always be careful not to actually *boil* the coffee and lose the flavour. It is therefore imperative that one personally watch over the pot to make sure that the water isn't boiling when it perks through the coffee, that grounds don't escape into the water, that the filter isn't clogged, and that percolation is no longer than six to eight minutes. Equally important is cleaning the pot thoroughly every day.

Coffee-maker, heated by kerosene burner, designed by Eickes circa 1930.

American espresso machine.

139

e. Espresso

The Italians are probably best known for their invention of the espresso coffee machine. Perfected in 1946, it is basically a means of extracting coffee's full flavour by *forcing* hot water at a pressure of four kilos per square centimetre through fine grounds (for an extraordinary concentration often exceeding the preferred 19 per cent extraction of soluble solids).

The machines, with their festoons of spigots, handles and gauges, could produce up to a thousand

cups an hour of strong, bitter but quite aromatic coffee. During the 1950's, espresso bars opened throughout Europe and America, where they became the equivalent of the 18th Century coffee-house: they were the most fashionable and exciting places for the young to gather.

More recent espresso machines are less flamboyant than the post-war marvels — but they are more respectful of the coffee and never over-extract its essence. One result is the use of such machines at home. The newest are steam-pressured and include the Pavoni,

Porcelain cone-shaped coffee filter, from Hamburg, circa 1910.

Ceramic cone-shaped coffee filter, from Hamburg, circa 1910.

Atomic and Vesuviana models, which are very expensive indeed.

Less expensive is the Moka Espresso. One separates top and base by unscrewing. The base is filled with water. The filter funnel has finely ground coffee. The top is screwed to the base and it is placed over the heat. As soon as the coffee begins to rise up to the top, the heat should be lowered to a minimum.

Once again, this is fairly satisfactory — except that if one does *not* watch the water carefully, and if the water rises *too* quickly, then one loses much of the flavour of the coffee.

f. Melitta and the perfect cup

Every coffee expert agrees that *filtered* coffee is the best way of preserving the most flavour and aroma in the most practical way. But it is only in the past 75 years that Melitta has *perfected* this filter to the point where the *maximum* flavour and aroma are brewed up in the most practical form.

To fully explain the Melitta method, a separate chapter is necessary.

Left: Pewter coffee filter, manufactured by G. Meurer Prua, 19th Century.

Below: Coffee filter with slit sieve, from Karlsbaden, circa 1900.

The Melitta revolution

Among more prominent landmarks in the history of coffee, the year 1908 stands out. This was the year when Frau Melitta Bentz invented a revolutionary new coffee-making process.

This was not a corporate decision. Frau Bentz was simply a housewife who wanted to please her hard-working husband, as well as her *Kaffeeklatsch* friends, with a coffee which had a good flavour but which didn't have grounds or bitter substances. Frau Bentz, like other coffee-lovers of her time, had put her ground coffee into a cloth bag and brewed it in the boiling water. Unfortunately, this meant that frequently the bag would wear out and coffee grounds were mixed in with the coffee. Or a *new* bag might be so secure that virtually none of the coffee flavour was extracted.

Like most inventors, Mrs. Bentz began with a simple idea, which only time improved. The idea was to *filter* the coffee. Her first experiments, with linen towels, were not totally successful. But when she put a simple sheet of blotting paper into a brass pot with a perforated bottom, she realised that her theory was correct. Pouring water just off the boil through the top, she produced the first filtered coffee.

The world has been a better place since then.

Frau Bentz' next step was to hire a tinsmith to produce these pots. Soon, the blotting paper was replaced by strong porous paper, which her two sons delivered to the enthusiastic neighbours. Within one year, though, at the Leipzig Trade Fair, no less than 1,250 aluminium coffee filter pots were sold. Mrs. Bentz' husband became manager of the company (which he named after his wife), and by 1912, Melitta was manufacturing its own filter.

In spite of its improvements, the Melitta theory remains the same. The Melitta system is simple, clean and convenient. It needs minimal maintenance. And it

Commemorative medallion.

142

Melitta's first filter.

efficiently extracts the optimum soluble coffee. Melitta separates the grounds from the brew, keeping out the undesirable oils and impurities, it is capable of producing fresh coffee for a single person or a large party. The result is that 84 per cent of German households use Melitta — with its fame and use spreading to 150 other countries.

The improvements which followed have been notable. First, during the 1930s, the disc-shaped filter top was replaced by the immediately identifiable Melitta mark, the cone-shape filter top. This was more than for aesthetic reasons, of course, for the surface area of the filter paper is increased two-and-a-half times, which means a far more effective utilisation of the filter-fine ground coffee.

Second, in 1940, an additional taste improvement was obtained by replacing the metal filter-top with porcelain, as porcelain cannot affect the flavour.

The world's best selling filter bags.

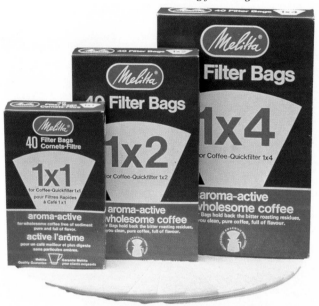

Third, the porcelain filter top is more and more being replaced by the plastic filter top: this is more economical, handier, and again, it doesn't affect the taste of the coffee.

Fourth, in 1966, the even more convenient so-called "1 × filter top" was on the market. This has an even larger filtering surface.

But the most important factor in the Melitta success story is the paper filter. Increasingly, in its own plant, Melitta improves the durability and permeability of its paper — and of course the purity of the paper is guaranteed.

Below: Melitta's filter top production.

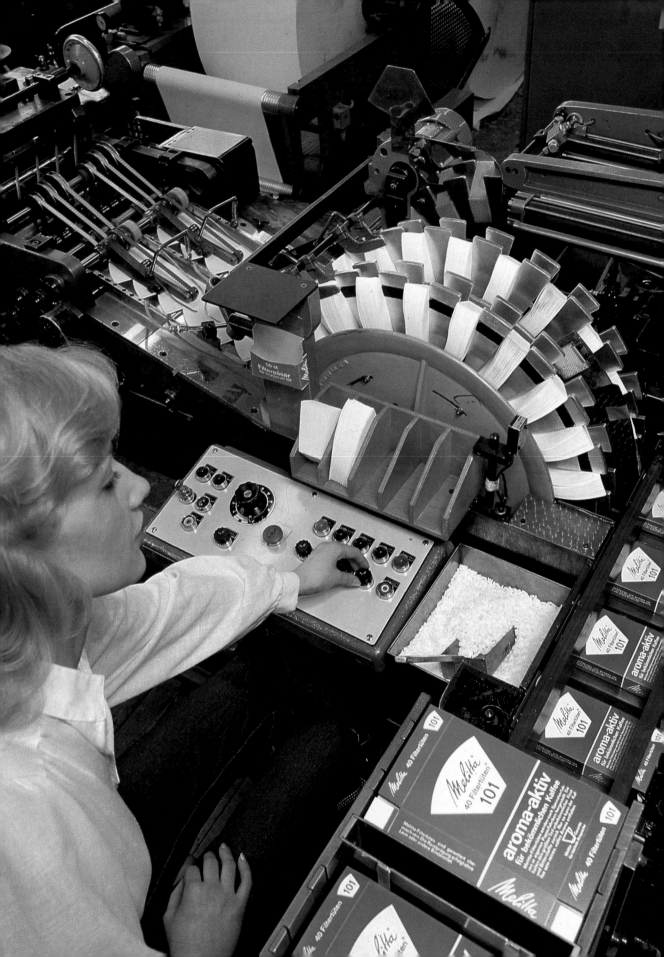

The result of this combination of established theory, steady improvement and paper is the automatic coffee-maker. The Melitta coffee-makers are all equipped with illuminated on-off switches, built-in warming plates, heat-resistant carafes and many different sizes. A superb cup of coffee is guaranteed with a simple four-step method.

1. Put the Melitta filter bag into the Melitta filter top.

2. Spoon in the required amount of coffee: about 1 Melitta measure per cup, or according to individual taste.

3. Moisten the coffee with boiling water, and allow it to soak for a few seconds to release the full flavour.

4. Add boiling water for the desired number of cups. The coffee will filter through automatically, and that "perfect cup" will result within a few minutes.

1.

2.

3.

4.

Herr Obrock: The joy of tasting.

But perfection is purely a personal matter. Melitta can make the coffee better and more economically: the taste, though, is up to the individual drinker.

In much of Asia, Europe and America, it would be impractical to blend one's own choice of coffee. Either the right beans aren't available, or they can't be guaranteed to have been roasted correctly, or the ratio of the blends isn't right. True, one *could* go to the trouble of importing the exact amount of coffee beans from around the world, roasting them oneself. But the difficulties for a single cup of coffee are almost insurmountable.

Melitta, though, has a very viable alternative. Rather than selling a

single blend of coffee, Melitta determines different blends with each sales region in mind. In other words, different markets prefer different blends.

The blending is supervised by one of the legendary figures of coffee, Herr Obrock of Bremen. Through Melitta, he has access to the world's finest beans, which he has been tasting and testing for decades. It is said that Herr Obrock can identify any place where coffee beans are grown. And he keeps a mental list of hundreds of different flavours and aromas.

The first step in the Melitta blends is to air-wash the beans of any residual impurities. Then Herr Obrock and/or his assistants control the blending process.

The next step is roasting. As Melitta has advanced internationally, roasting plants have multiplied. Presently, plants aren't only in Germany, but in Brazil, the United States, Japan and France. Each plant is supervised by the Melitta Roast Master, who constantly observes and controls the coffee. The roasting is determined by computer, and by a specially-designed colour chart.

From the roaster, the beans go directly through a special pipe to the grinder, where the beans are cut to exactly the right grind for the Melitta filter. After cutting, the beans are left for 7-8 minutes, so the carbon dioxide formed during roasting can be diffused gradually out of the bean. Once the bean is de-gassed, Melitta encloses the coffee in air-tight bags and tins. To ensure freshness, Melitta packages its coffee within 60 minutes of roasting.

The beans themselves come from the best coffee countries in the world. From Brazil comes Santos, the fine all-round coffee for breakfast, lunch or dinner. Certainly the most "rounded" coffee. From Guatemala come mild and mellow blends with a high acidity and the best bouquet. From Kenya comes the Peaberry bean with its excellent flavour, body and acidity. From Tanzania comes a bean similar to Kenya but with a sharper winey quality. From Jamaica comes that wonderful rare mild coffee, which, like Blue Mountain, never goes to extremes. And from Ethiopia, Melitta brings forth the chocolatey Mocha coffee to add a richness found in no other bean.

Over the past three-quarters of a century, Melitta has never let its standards fall. Quite the opposite: as Melitta has remained in the same family since its founding, so the company has expanded only in terms of an all-inclusive comprehensive coffee "philosophy". All of the products from Melitta are interrelated to give — as much as possible — the perfect cup of coffee.

Coffee-lovers in countries where coffee has been brewed with older methods, say the Melitta system creates coffee too mechanically, that it is *too* perfect, that it detracts from the ritual of making coffee.

That is absolutely true. For those places where the long, slow, haphazard ritual is more important than . . . well, more important than the cup of coffee itself, Melitta may not be suitable. But for those looking for flexibility, economy, time-saving, and most of all, for a cup of coffee which can always be dependable, then Melitta with the cone filter, in the automatic machines and/or the blends — is the greatest boon for coffee-loving mankind.

149

L'envoi

How do I drink thee? Let me
count the ways.
I drink thee for the taste and
scent and roast
My senses feel. And ever more
engrossed,
For time alone improves thy fine
bouquets.
The memories of coffee nights and
days
Are pure solace: if by myself, my cup
Becomes my confidante, my
lover and my host;
With friends, small rooms are
Mozart-filled *cafés*.
With thee, the world and history
are unconfined:
To Mocha first I soar, then Java
and Versailles;
To King and Pope and Sultan: all
mankind
Has supped of thee, thy praise to
amplify.
So rich, so gentle and so designed,
That thee and thy world
should mutually glorify.

Attributed to Elizabeth Barrett
Roasting (*neé* Browning).

The world
of coffee

Landau's Coffee (one portion)

Ingredients:
1 teaspoon	brown sugar
20 g	creme de cacao
20 g	anisette
120 g	hot strong coffee
30 g	fresh cream — whipped
4 teaspoon	sugar — caramel

Preparation:
Melt sugar in flambe pan to a
golden brown caramel. Dip the
rim of the coffee glass into the
caramel and let it run down
the outside of the glass and let
it cool.
Spoon the brown sugar into
the glass, add the creme de
cacao and anisette and stir.
Fill up with the hot coffee
until a quarter-inch under the
rim and top with whipped
fresh cream.

Marnissimo

Pour into a glass a measure of
Grand Marnier Cordon Rouge and
a good cup of your favourite
Melitta blend, add sugar to taste
and stir well. Top with fresh
cream so that it floats on the
surface. Serve — taking care that
the cream does not mix with the
liquid.

the coffee and gently bring back to the boil. Remove the orange, flambe in a soup ladle with 6 cl Cognac, then refloat in the coffee.

Sherry Coffee Punch (Serves 8)

48 g	Melitta coffee
1/5 l	cream sherry
1 pc	orange peel, grated
1 stick	cinnamon
8 cubes	sugar
4 tbsp	dark rum

Preparation:
Prepare the coffee in the Melitta coffee-maker with 1 litre of water. Add the sherry, orange peel and cinnamon and gently bring back to the boil. Fill the cups. For each cup, take a sugar cube in a pair of tongs, soak with rum and flambe.

Cafe Diable (Serves 8)

48 g	Melitta coffee
1	orange
20	cloves
1 pc	orange peel
1 pc	lemon peel
2 sticks	cinnamon
10 cubes	sugar
15 cl	Cognac
6 cl	Cognac (for flambe)

Preparation:
Prepare the coffee in the Melitta coffee-maker with 1 litre of water and set aside. Lard the orange with the cloves, add with the orange peel, lemon peel, cinnamon and sugar to 15 cl Cognac in a heat-resistant bowl and heat until sugar melts. Add

Kaffee Kahn

Kaffee Kahn (Serves 6)

Praline Parfait

Ingredients:
6	coconut halves
5	egg yolks
120 g	sugar
100 g	praline paste
500 g	fresh whipped cream

Preparation:
Whip up the egg yolks and sugar.
Fold together with the whipped
egg yolks and sugar, the praline
paste and the fresh whipped
cream.
Half fill the coconut shells with
the praline parfait and place in
the freezer until hard (2-3 hours).

'Coffeecream'

Ingredients:
300 g	fresh soft whipped cream
36 g	Melitta coffee
150 cl	Kahlua coffee liqueur

Preparation:
Prepare the coffee in your Melitta
coffee-maker, with only a little
water. Mix the ingredients
together well, but not for too long.
For people who prefer an
Espresso taste, add more Melitta
coffee.

The Flambé

Ingredients:
3	bananas
60 g	butter
60 g	sugar
6 cl	Kahlua
9 cl	Cognac
3	chopped pistachio nuts
18	coffee beans

Preparation:
Cut the bananas into small cubes
and sauté with the butter in a hot
copper pan (sauté quickly,
otherwise the bananas will
become too soft). Lower the heat
and sprinkle with the sugar and
the Kahlua (keep them warm in a
dish). Use the copper pan again to
heat up the Cognac and set
alight. Add the prepared bananas
and heat up.
Place the half coconut shells on a
dessert plate and pour in the
banana flambé. Cover with the
coffeecream and decorate with the
coffee beans and chopped
pistachio nuts.

Mocca Tart

Sponge:
4	egg yolks
150 g	sugar
4	egg whites
100 g	flour
25 g	cornstarch
1 tsp	baking powder
25 g	vanilla sugar
2-3 tsp	warm water
2 tbsp	fresh-brewed Melitta coffee

Filling:
250 g	butter
200 g	dark chocolate
5	egg yolks
150 g	icing sugar
2 cl	brandy
2 tbsp	strong filter Melitta coffee; one bag of Mocca beans

Preparation and cooking:
Whip the egg yolks and water, add 100g sugar and vanilla sugar and beat until foaming. Beat the egg whites and 50g sugar until stiff. Bring the egg yolks and egg whites together, fold in remaining sponge ingredients and mix well. Line a baking tin with baking paper, add the mixture and bake in an oven, preheated to 200°C, for about 40 minutes, take out the tin and leave to cool.

Filling:
Whip the butter until creamy. Melt the chocolate in a double-boiler, add the egg yolks, sugar and coffee, blend well and leave to cool. Add the butter and mix well, folding in the brandy, then set a small amount aside.
Slice the sponge into 3 layers of equal thickness. Spread filling thickly on 1st layer, add 2nd layer and repeat, then add 3rd layer. Decorate top with remaining filling and several Mocca beans and decorate sides with one tbsp Melitta coffee powder.

Bisquit Coffee

In a three-quarter full cup of good
coffee, pour slowly the contents of
one glass of Bisquit VSOP making
it slide along a tea spoon which
will just be in contact with the
coffee surface. Bisquit Cognac will
float on the surface and will make
your drink most tasty and enjoy-
able. If you like your Bisquit
coffee very hot, you can flame it.

Coffeeshake (Serves 6)

36 g	Melitta coffee
2 tsp	cocoa powder
2 tbsp	sugar
¼ l	milk
1/8 l	fresh cream
	grated chocolate

Preparation:
Prepare the coffee in the Melitta coffee-maker with ¾ litre of water and leave to cool. Add the cocoa powder, sugar and milk and blend well. Fill 6 glasses, top with whipped fresh cream and sprinkle with chocolate.

Vanilla-Orange Coffee (Serves 4)

24 g	Melitta coffee
75 g	sugar
	fresh juice of 2 oranges
1	orange, peeled and diced
2 cl	orange liqueur
4 scoops	vanilla ice cream

Preparation:
Prepare the coffee in the Melitta coffee-maker with ½ litre of water, add the sugar and leave to cool. Add the orange juice and mix. Marinate the diced orange in the liqueur, divide equally between 4 glasses, then add a scoop of ice cream to each. Fill the glasses with the coffee and decorate with slices of orange.

163

Iced Coffee 'Olé'

36 g	Melitta coffee
200 g	honey melon, cleaned and diced
30 g	sugar
6 cl	Kirsch
1/8 l	fresh cream cocoa powder

Preparation:
Prepare the coffee in the Melitta coffee-maker with ¾ litre of water and leave to cool. Mix the melon and sugar and add with the Kirsch to the coffee. Chill in the refrigerator freezer compartment for about 15 minutes. Pour into long glasses, top with whipped fresh cream, sprinkle with cocoa power and serve.

Cafe du Roi (Serves 4)

4 measures	Melitta Coffee
½ l	Champagne (sec or demi-sec)
2 sticks	cinnamon

Preparation:
Warm 4 glasses and add ½ stick
cinnamon to each. Prepare the
coffee in the Melitta manual
coffee-maker, using Champagne
instead of water. Fill the glasses
and let stand for 5-8 minutes
before serving.

Star Tart with Coffee Cream Filling

Sponge A:

125 g	butter or margarine
75 g	sugar
25 g	vanilla sugar
100 g	flour
50 g	cornstarch
2 tsp	baking powder
2	eggs
pinch	salt

Sponge B:

75 g	nut nougat
40 g	chopped almonds
1 tsp	powdered ginger
1 tbsp	cocoa powder
1 tbsp	dark rum
3 tbsp	raspberry spirit
2 tbsp	raspberry jam

Filling:

	fresh cream
2 tbsp	fresh-brewed Melitta coffee
pinch	powdered cinnamon

Glazing:

250 g	icing sugar
1 tsp	powdered cinnamon
1 tbsp	fresh-brewed Melitta coffee
2-3 tbsp	hot water

Decoration: coffee beans

Preparation and cooking:
Whip the butter or margarine until creamy, add remaining sponge A ingredients and mix thoroughly. Mix in sponge B ingredients. Line a star-shaped baking tin with baking paper, add the mixture and bake in an oven, preheated to 175°C, for about 60 minutes.

Allow the sponge to cool, then slice into 3 layers of equal thickness. Sprinkle 1st and 2nd layers with raspberry spirit and spread with raspberry jam. Stir the filling ingredients in a saucepan over a low flame (do not allow to cook). Leave to cool, then whip until stiff. Set a small amount aside, spread filling thickly on 1st layer, add 2nd layer and repeat, then add 3rd layer. Mix hot water with glazing ingredients, glaze the tart and leave to cool. Decorate with remaining filling and several Mocca beans.

Cherry Mocca Waffles (Makes 4)

Waffles:
250 g	butter
100 g	sugar
25 g	vanilla sugar
4	eggs
200 g	flour
50 g	cornstarch
2 tsp	baking powder

Filling:
½ glass	nut nougat cream
2-3 tbsp	strong fresh-brewed Melitta coffee
1 tbsp	dark rum
1 glass	cherries

Preparation and cooking:
Whip the butter, sugar and vanilla sugar until creamy, add the eggs, then fold in the remaining waffle ingredients and mix well. Using a waffle maker, bake 8 waffles.
Thoroughly mix the cream, coffee and rum, spread thickly on 4 waffles and top with the cherries. Cover with remaining waffles and serve.

Cream Horns

300 g	puff pastry mixture
1	egg yolk
2 tbsp	crystal sugar

Filling:
250 g	baker's cheese
2 tbsp	nut nougat cream
2 tbsp	sugar

Glazed Peaches

8 tbsp	canned peach halves
1 tbsp	Kirsch
1/6 l	fresh cream
2 tbsp	strong fresh-brewed Melitta coffee
2 tbsp	sugar
pinch	powdered cinnamon
250 g	fresh raspberries

Preparation and cooking:
Sprinkle the peaches with Kirsch.
Whip the cream and mix in the
coffee, sugar and cinnamon.
Layer the bottom of an oven-proof
dish with half the cream, add the
peaches (inside uppermost), cover
with remaining cream and glaze
in a very hot oven. Decorate the
centre of each peach with
raspberries and serve.

3 tbsp	strong fresh-brewed Melitta coffee

Preparation and cooking:
Cut aluminium foil into circles of
about 30 cm diameter. Cut each
circle into half, form the halves
into cones and stuff each cone
with greaseproof paper. Roll out
the pastry mixture, cut into
strips and wind around each
aluminium foil cone. Brush with
egg yolk, sprinkle with the
crystal sugar and bake in an
oven, preheated to 200°C, for
about 15 minutes. Remove the
aluminium foil cones and leave
the pastry cones to cool.
Thoroughly mix the filling
ingredients and insert a generous
amount into each pastry cone.

Autumn Coffee

24 g	Melitta Coffee
2 cl	dark rum
2 cl	Grand Marnier
2 cl	syrup
1 tbsp	whipped cream
2	ice cubes

Preparation:
Prepare the coffee in the Melitta
coffee maker with ½ litre of
water, add the ice cubes and leave
to cool. Mix in the rum, Grand
Marnier and syrup. Pour into
glasses, top with cream and serve.

Appendices

The derivation of the name coffee

While the origin of coffee is fairly well established as being Ethiopia, there is no definitive answer to the derivation of the word itself. "Coffee" itself appeared in English and French around 1600, when travellers described that "black brew" which the heathens were drinking. At that time, it was thought to come from the Turkish word *kahveh*, which (it is still said by scholars) came from the word *caouhe*, a kind of seed which either resembled coffee or was coffee itself. The seed may have been related to a grape, for coffee was thought of as a wine of sorts in Turkey. Another theory takes the Arabic word *cahoueh* or *gwaweh*, which means "to give vigour or strength." It is said that this too was later transformed into "coffee"

Possibly the most rational and plainest theory is that the word "coffee" comes from its place of origin in Ethiopia. In Ethiopia itself, coffee was originally called "bunn." But this was prior to its discovery in the rest of the Middle East. The province of Kaffa, in South Western Ethiopia, was an independent kingdom until the late 19th century. Here, coffee trees grew wild in ancient times as they grow wild today. It seems likely that, once coffee reached the Arabian peninsula, its place of origin (as well as Kaffa, the *language* of the area) gave its name to the coffee plant.

After that, Arabic words could have been appended to the mundane geographical explanation.

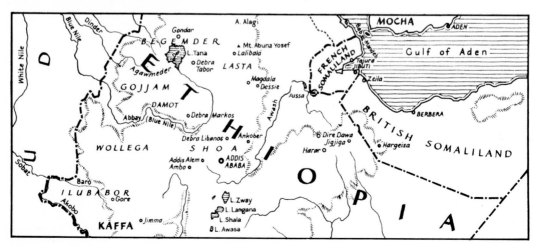

Coffee and health

Oscar Wilde said, "Each man kills the thing he loves." Mankind has loved coffee for so long that he has long felt that coffee just *couldn't* be as good and healthful and as stimulating as it's supposed to be. So through the ages, there have been as many sceptics as advocates on the health value of coffee.

In the Middle Ages, opinion was divided in the Middle East. One great Arab philosopher and doctor praised coffee for being the panacea against high blood pressure, smallpox and measles, as well as being a stimulant. On the other hand, one Persian sage told about the effects of coffee on the Prophet Mohammed when delivered to him by the Angel Gabriel: "He felt able to unseat 40 horsemen and possess 50 women."

Then there were the naysayers. In 1511, at a great "coffee trial," two Persian brothers testified that coffee was indeed injurious to the health — but it was later revealed that the Hakimani brothers, quacks of the worst sort, were ready to sell their "knowledge" to the highest bidder.

The great Turkish writer, Hajji Khalifah wrote in his *Mizan al-Hacc* (The Balance Of Truth), around 1635, a rather fair-minded comment: "By its 'dryness,' coffee repels sleep. It has a positive diuretic effect, varying with the temperament. To those of dry temperament, especially to the man of melancholic temperament, large quantities are unsuitable and may be repugnant. Taken in excess, it causes insomnia and melancholic anxiety. To those of moist temperament, and especially to women, it is highly suited. They should drink a great deal of strong coffee. Excess of it will do them no harm, so long as they are not melancholic."

An excellent diagnosis for its time. Of a rather unscientific thesis though is Khalifah's comment that "Coffee is cold and dry. Even when it is boiled in water and an infusion made of it, its coldness does not depart. Perhaps it increases, for water too is cold. That is why coffee quenches thirst, and does not burn if poured on a limb, for its heat is a strange heat with no effect."

In the 18th Century, it was praised by some, called "a slow poison" by others. In the 19th Century, an American advertisement called coffee "The tree of health," implying it as a veritable elixir.

That, of course, is nonsense.

175

Coffee does have definite values — certainly in stimulating the mind — and its diuretic qualities are well known. But as an actual medicinal aid . . . that's going too far.

The secret of coffee stimulation is caffeine, a complex chemical which is only now being properly analysed. Everyone knows that it stimulates and can keep people awake. But it has also been proven that caffeine can soothe to sleep by arousing the circulation to carry more oxygen to the brain. Caffeine also counters depression and so eases the mind. In Scandinavia, coffee is drunk right at bedtime in order to promote good sleep.

In 1970, Dr. J. Murdoch Ritchie wrote of caffeine in *The Pharmacological Basis of Therapeutics*. Caffeine, he said, produces "a more rapid and clearer flow of thought," allaying "drowsiness and fatigue. After taking caffeine, one is capable of a greater sustained intellectual effort and a more perfect association of ideas. There is also a keener appreciation of sensory stimuli and motor activity is increased."

Of course, caffeine can also produce "coffee nerves" if taken in too large a dose. But like everything else, coffee should be taken in moderation for its best effect.

With caffeine, everyone has a personal level in tolerance. Within one cup of coffee are about 100 milligrams of caffeine. No negative effects have ever been felt by anyone consuming even

Typical Ethiopian banquet which always ended with coffee.

300 milligrams. So one should be able to drink at least five cups a day with no ill effects.

But individuals vary considerably. Some could actually be allergic to coffee. Others, especially writers and similar stellar souls, drink up to 30 cups a day with no ill effects at all.

On other positive notes, it has been proven that both caffeine and chlorogenic acid, contained in coffee, have cancer-preventing properties. Chlorogenic acid is also an anti-oxidant which slows down the ageing processes. This might account for some longevity records among coffee drinkers like Voltaire and Elizabeth Durieux, who took as many as 40 cups a day during most of her 114 years on earth.

The vitamin niacin is another valuable component of coffee. Lack of niacin affects the metabolism of the gastric and intestinal area. One cup of coffee contains a daily requirement of the vitamin.

Coffee does more than stimulate the body psychologically. It actually does stimulate circulation, though it doesn't increase the blood pressure or affect the heart. The lindic acids in coffee oils are believed to help clotting of the blood and thrombosis. It is non-fattening and can safely be drunk by all.

Decaffeinated coffee appeals to a certain kind of coffee-lover. Those with sensitive stomachs, those who find coffee over-stimulating, or those who are afraid that a coffee 'nightcap'' will ruin their sleep may prefer to drink the decaffeinated coffee.

Caffeine itself does nothing for the aroma of coffee, and virtually nothing for the flavour. (The crystalline substance has only the slightest bitter taste). The real problem is how to take caffeine out from the coffee bean without removing the rest of the substances which do influence coffee flavour.

Fortunately, with modern decaffeination processes, freshly roasted decaffeinated coffee, properly ground and brewed, can taste so close to "untreated" coffee that only a tasting involving direct comparison will reveal the difference.

The extraction process begins by soaking the green unroasted coffee beans under high steam pressure. Then, a volatile non-toxic caffeine solvent is flushed through the swollen beans carrying away the caffeine. Final steam flushing removes the surplus solvent. At that point the green beans are subject to the meticulous and careful roasting which gives coffee its characteristic aroma and flavour.

177

Key people and words in coffee

Abd-al-Kadir, Sheikh: 16th Century Arab writer on coffee.

Acid, acidy, acidity: Interchangeable words; the usually pleasant bitterness in coffee, resulting from acids formed in roasting. Thus, light roasts have more acid than dark roasted coffee.

Arabica: One of the two major coffee genii, named (falsely) from its alleged Arabic origins. The finest coffees are made from Arabica.

Aroma: Not just the smell of coffee, but an integral part of the flavour. Over 300 chemical changes take place, and some of the aroma components still have not been analysed.

Avicenna: Arabic physician and writer who extolled the values of coffee in the 10th Century.

Bach, Johann Sebastian: 18th Century composer of the *Coffee Cantata*. Some say that after this "Bach's breakfast" music, he was preparing a *"Sandwich Cantata"* as a "Bach's lunch."

Backgammon: Ancient game, originally as much a part of a Middle Eastern coffee-house as coffee itself.

Barnyard fermented: One of the adjectives used by professional coffee-tasters. For others, see chapter on tasting.

Body: The "heaviness" of coffee in the mouth.

Boston Tea Party: 18th Century American protest at British tea-taxes, when tea imported by the the British from Macau was thrown in Boston harbour. It became practically subversive to drink tea, making the United States a coffee-drinking country.

Brewing: Running hot water through coffee grounds to bring out the flavour, aroma, colour and body. It is not cooking.

Cafe Procope: The most famous coffee-house of 18th century France.

Caffeine: An alkaloid in coffee (and tea), which, according to one book, produces "a more rapid and clearer flow of thought." In the more expensive brands, there is less caffeine than in the instants.

Caffeol: The volatile complex from roasting which produces aroma.

Capuccino: Style of coffee with one third espresso, one third hot milk, topped with foam, powdered with cinnamon or nutmeg.

Cardamom: Middle Eastern spice frequently used in coffee.

Chicory: A herb whose powdered roots are sometimes added to coffees to cheapen the price. In Belgium, chicory is actually appreciated.

Coffee-houses: More than for drinking coffee, the coffee-houses were traditionally clubs, where men would come together and discuss everything from politics to . . . . well, to coffee.

Cona (also Kona): A method of brewing coffee similar to the vacuum method. Made in two bowls. Also Hawaiian coffee.

Crust test: In coffee-tasting, breaking the top crust on a cup and getting the first aroma.

Decaffeination: The process of removing up to 99.9 per cent of caffeine through a special high-pressure steam soaking process.

Decoction: The earliest method of making coffee: boiling the grounds directly until the flavour is extracted (see *infusion*)

Drip pot: Old French method of brewing coffee; the *café filtre* is a modern version. Basically, a three-part pot of water receiver, coffee basket and beverage receiver.

Drying method: One of two methods of getting coffee beans ready for the roaster. Here, the beans are left to dry in the sun for up to three weeks. Not as effective as "washing" (q.v.).

Espresso: Post-World War II method of making coffee by forcing steam at high pressure through beans, extracting more from them than boiling water. High roast is always recommended.

Filter: Most economical method of brewing coffee, with the soluble material coming through the filter paper.

Frederick the Great: King of Prussia 1740-86. Excellent flute-player but anaethema to coffee-lovers, for a) banning coffee for commoners; b) frequently preparing his own coffee with champagne rather than water!

Freeze-drying: A complex but more palatable way of manufacturing instant coffee. It is no substitute for *real* coffee, of course, but it is basically potable. Chemical additives are obvious negative factors.

Garboon: Spittoon used by professional New York coffee-tasters.

Goldoni: Italian dramatist (1707-93). Among his 150 comedies, his *Coffee-House* is one of the most popular.

Green coffee: Two distinct meanings. a) Unroasted coffee. b) In New York, the price of coffee, in commodities markets.

Grinding: After roasting the coffee bean, the bean is ground, releasing its aroma and flavour. For the numerous grinders and grades of grinding, see *The Ground's The Limit*.

Hacienda: Brazilian plantation.

Ibrik. The decocting Turkish coffee-pot. A small long-handled pot in which coffee is boiled directly over the stove.

Infusion: One of the two methods of making coffee. Here, heated water passes through the grounds, extracting soluble material.

Java: Slang term for coffee, especially in United States, probably because Dutch coffee was the first imported in America when it was a Dutch possession.

Today, it usually stands for Indonesian coffees, though the finest are not raised on Java, but Sumatra.

Kaffeeklatsch: German for "coffee-gossip," the feminine equivalent of the coffee-house, where women could share the "aristocratic" drink with their friends.

Khaldi: The legendary goat-herder who brought coffee beans to a monastery, starting its popularity in religious circles.

Kolschitzky, Franz George: Founder of the first Viennese coffee-house, from grounds seized by fleeing Turkish troops in the 17th Century.

Liberica: One of the two major brands of coffee. Inferior to Arabica (q.v.), but hardier. Indigenous to West Africa.

Liqueur: Alcoholic spirits, many varieties of which are made with coffee.

Maragogipe: A mutant variety of Arabica, producing very large beans.

Melitta filter: The cone-shaped filter which revolutionised the coffee industry through making coffee economically, with no grounds, and with a far greater soluble material extracted.

Mocha: Originally, the port town in Yemen from which Mocha coffee (transplanted from Ethiopia) came. Today, Mocha is a type of chocolatey coffee which rarely is exported from Yemen, and is more likely to come from Ethiopia.

Napier Vacuum Pump: The first fully-developed filtration system, invented in 1840 by Scottish engineer Robert Napier.

Omar, Sheikh: The Moslem teacher who brought the coffee bean to Yemen and spread its popularity throughout the countryside.

Peaberry: (also known as *caracol*): A small grade of bean, occurring in every country.

Percolator: The coffee-pot where water is pumped up through a stem, filtering through the coffee, extracting flavour and aroma and returning to the pot below. The word comes from the Latin *percolatus*, meaning "to filter through."

Point: In tasting, the "sharpness" which one sometimes tastes. Too much and it can become unpleasant; too little, and some of the good coffee bitterness is gone.

Pope Clement VIII: The 16th Century Father of the Church who approved coffee for non-Moslems, a very Christian act indeed.

Roasting: The only actual cooking for the coffee. During the roasting period, certain natural chemicals are destroyed and others are created, giving the unique flavour, aroma, colour and feel of coffee.

Robusta: The cheapest coffee beans, usually used only in instant coffees.

Ruiacea: The Latin name for the coffee plant.

Santos: Brazilian coffee, so probably the most famous in the world. Other coffees have certain remarkable attributes. i.e. the aroma of Blue Mountain or the chocolatey texture of Mocha. But only Santos (or at least the better grades of Santos) is synonymous with coffee. A rounded coffee, with mild flavour, good aroma, moderate acidity. The best grade is Bourbon Santos, which comes from the original Arabica coffee planted in the 18th Century. After three or four years, Bourbon Santos loses some of its finest qualities and becomes a little flat. This coffee is called "flat bean Santos," but is usually sold simply as Santos.

Strength: In coffee, strength does *not* refer to flavour. It refers to the ratio of coffee to water. With more coffee and less water, the brew is stronger. A light-roasted mild-flavoured coffee can be stronger than a dark-roasted sharp-flavoured coffee.

Twain, Mark: American writer (1835-1910) who loved his coffee and his travel and had the most pungent comments to make about coffees he tasted all over the world.

Valorisation: The method by which different countries try to regulate coffee prices, buying up the crop and keeping it until prices are adjusted. It has never worked well, because different competing countries have rarely cooperated fully, and smuggling is frequently uncontrolled.

Voltaire: French philosopher (1694-1778) who scoffed at the very idea of coffee doing any harm to the physiology or cerebral processes. As the living example, Voltaire would drink up to 50 cups a day — and he survived for 84 very happy, very productive years.

Washing (Wet method): One of the two methods of drying beans, preparing them to go from the plantation to the market. More efficient than the dry method (but also more costly). The hand-picked beans are washed, then put into machines to remove the pulp. Then the beans are left to ferment, washed again and left to dry, after which hulling machines take away the toughest part of the beans. With the thorough fermentation process and more careful picking, "washed" coffees are finer and more expensive than "dry" coffees.

Winey: A kind of wine after-taste found in some of the more acidic coffees.

The saga of coffee

Coffee history	Year
First wild coffee eaten, in Africa	6th Century A.D.:
Legend of Khaldi the goatherd and discovery of coffee's properties	Circa 850 A.D.:
Avicenna describes coffee's medicinal properties	910:
Coffee first roasted and boiled	11th Century:
Coffee prepared from dry bean hulls	12th Century:
First Middle Eastern coffee-houses	14th Century:
Governor of Mecca bans coffee-houses	1511:
First coffee-house in Oxford	1560:
First mention of coffee in a European book	1573:
Arab poem composed to coffee	1587:
Pope Clement VIII blesses coffee brought to Italy	Circa 1594:
Coffee first mentioned in United Kingdom	1599:
First coffee seeds smuggled to India	1600:
Captain John Smith introduces coffee to the New World	1607:
First coffee is brought to Oxford	1637:
First coffee cultivated in Ceylon	1658:
First published coffee recipes in England	1662:
First coffee in New York	1668:
Turkish Ambassador to Paris holds fashionable parties, making coffee the "toast of France."	1669:
Charles II bans coffee-houses, but rescinds order immediately	1675:
Turks defeated in Vienna: hero of battle opens first Viennese coffee-house	1683:
First coffee cultivation in Java	1690:
Opening of Cafe Procope in Paris	Circa 1700:
First "cheap" coffee for Paris proletariat	1710:

World events

- Byzantine Empire; Goths overrun Europe
- Rise of feudalism in Western Europe and Japan

- Beginning of Fatamist Dynasty in North Africa, which would conquer much of Europe
- End of the world prophesied for Christianity
- First Shogunate set up in feudal Japan
- Chaucer writes *Canterbury Tales;* music composed by Machaut

- Henry VIII marries his first wife; Michaelangelo begins Sistine Chapel
- Height of slave trade on Africa's West Coast; birth of Nell Gwynn
- Spanish begin colonisation of Philippines; birth of dramatist Ben Jonson and architect Inigo Jones
- Shah Abbas I of Iran begins reign
- Shakespeare writes *Richard III*
- Birth of painter Velasquez
- British East India Company chartered for trade

- Jamestown founded in America (by Captain Smith); Ben Jonson completes *Volpone*
- Dutch begin to occupy Ceylon
- King Louis XIV grants Moliere permanent theatre in Paris
- K'ang Hsi begins reign in China; Philosopher Blaise Pascal dies in France
- Birth of composer Couperin
- Death of Rembrandt

- Sir Christopher Wren begins building St. Paul's Cathedral

- Birth of composer Jean-Philippe Rameau

- First American newspaper, in Boston
- Russians, Poles and Danish fight Sweden for Baltic supremacy

- Addison and Steele prepare first edition of *Spectator* newspaper

183

Coffee history	Year
Coffee tree presented to King Louis XIV, father of all coffee	1713:
First coffee in West Indies	1720:
First coffee-house in Berlin	1721:
First coffee tasted in Japan	1724:
First coffee tree planted in Brazil	1727:
Bach's *Coffee Cantata*	1732:
Linnaeus dubs the plant *Coffea Arabica*	1735:
Boston Tea Party, making America a coffee-drinking country	1773:
Frederick the Great bans coffee for commoners	1777:
"Coffee-house" French Revolution	1789:
First percolator used	1800:
Pumping percolator invented	1827:
Napier Vacuum System invented	1840:
Cultivation of coffee in India	1840:
Coffee crop wiped out in Ceylon	1869:
Indian coffee crop wiped out	1870:
Wild *robusta* coffee found in Africa	1870:
First coffee trade association	1888:
Discovery of decaffeination	1900:
Instant-coffee theory developed in Guatamala	1906:
Frau Melitta Bentz experiments with filters for revolutionary coffee-making	1908:
Stock market crash, bringing coffee market to lowest level	1929:
Italian espresso coffee machine perfected	1946:
International Coffee Agreement signed to control market	1959:
Freeze-dried coffee developed	1960's:

- Reign of Frederick William I, King of Prussia

- G.F. Handel premieres opera, *Radamisto*, in London
- Paraguay becomes first state in South America to revolt against Spain
- English build first permanent settlement in Vermont
- Accession of King George II in England
- Benjamin Franklin begins publication of *Poor Richard's Almanack*
- Reign of Emperor Ch'ien Lung, when China maximises its territory
- Peasant rebellion in Russia

- Captain James Cook visits Tasmania
- George Washington inaugurated as first American President
- Election of Pope Pius VII in Vatican. John Adams elected second U.S. President

- Death of composer Ludwig van Beethoven
- Birth of Tchaikovsky
- British and Chinese involved in "Opium Wars"
- Rights given American blacks to vote
- Congo River explored by Henry Stanley
- Death of Charles Dickens and Alexandre Dumas
- Cecil Rhodes gets monopoly on diamonds in East Africa; George Bernard Shaw begins work as music critic
- Ibn Saud begins conquest of Arabia: Oscar Wilde dies

- U.K. launches first large battleship, starting world-wide naval buildup
- Birth of Dmitri Shostakovitch, death of Henrik Ibsen; William Howard Taft elected President of United States
- Vatican City declared separate from Italy in Lateran Agreement; ballet producer Serge Diaghelev dies
- Philippines granted independence from United States
- Fidel Castro comes to power in Cuba

- The era of assassinations, the Beatles and fast food chains commences

World coffee facts and figures

Country • Port(s) of shipping	Total harvested 1980 / 81 • Total exported 1980 / 81 (1000's of 60 kg. Sacks)	Kind of coffee • Drying method
AFRICA		
ANGOLA • Cabina, Luanda	350 • 265	Robusta, Ganada Arabica • Drying
BURUNDI • Dar Es Salaam, Mombassa	333 • 330	Arabica 3pc Robusta
CAMEROONS • Douala, Victoria	1,680 • 1,618	Arabica (Sept-Nov) Robusta (Nov-Feb) • Washed (Arabica) Dried (Robusta)
CENTRAL AFRICAN REP. • Pointe Noire	235 • 218	Robusta, some Excelsa • Dried
COMOROS* • Maroni		Robusta • Dried
DAHOMEY (BENIN) • Cotonou	★	Robusta • Dried
EQUATORIAL GUINEA • Bata, Santa Isabel	100 • 90	Liberica, Robusta • Dried
ETHIOPIA • Djibouti, Assab, Massawa	3,100 • 1,250	Arabica • Washed / Dried
GABON • Libreville	★	Robusta • Dried
GHANA • Accra	★	Robusta • Dried
GUINEA • Conakry	★	Robusta some Arabica • Dried
IVORY COAST • Abidjan	4,500 • 4,435	Robusta, Excelsa, Liber, "Inden" • Mainly dry
KENYA • Mombassa	1,250 • 1,194	Arabica • Washed
LIBERIA • Monrovia	135 • 123	Robusta, Liberica
MALAGASY (Madagascar) • Vohemar, other ports	1,500 • 1,334	Robusta some Arabica • Dried, some washed
NIGERIA • Lagos	★	Robusta some Arabica • Dried
RWANDA • Matadi, Dar Es Salaam, Mombassa	527 • 525	Arabica • Washed
SIERRA LEONE • Freetown	180 • 175	Robusta, Liberica • Dried

186

Important Grades	Notes
Ambriz	Pleasant filler for U.S. blends
AAA-BBB	AAA (80 pc) rich, acid. BBB is undrinkable
Elephant	Mellow, sweet
Harrar, Shortberry, Longberry, Djimmash, Sidamos	Top grades, great body, acid, winy, superb Mocha type. Last two grades excellent for blending with heavier blends like Colombian, Java
I.C. Robusta	I.C. supplies 8 per cent of world's Robustas for blending. Most grown on small farms, not plantations.
AA-BB	Mild, declicate, acid, smooth. A's are smooth, B's unpleasantly sharp
	The home of Liberica wild coffee.
	Mainly Robusta for instant coffee.
FWAAA, FWAA, FWA 1, 2, 3a, 3b, 4, 5.	Fully washed strong, high acidity, rich. Best go to Europe. "Washed" go to US.
	Coarse, used mainly in instant blends.

Country • Port(s) of shipping	Total harvested 1980 / 81 • Total exported 1980 / 81 (1000's of 60 kg. Sacks)	Kind of coffee • Drying method
TANZANIA • Dar Es Salaam, Tanga, Mombassa	860 • 835	Arabica (66 pc), Robusta, (34 pc) AA, A, B • Washed and dried
TOGO • Lome	160 • 159	Robusta (Niaouli) • Dried
UGANDA • Mombassa	2,000 • 1,970	Robusta, some Arabica • Dried / Washed
ZAIRE • Matadi, Mombassa	1,400 • 1,205	Robusta (83pc), Arabica (17pc)

LATIN AMERICA

BOLIVIA • Arica, Matarni	145 • 111	Arabica • Washed
BRAZIL • Paranagua, Santos, Rio de Janeiro, Recife, many other ports	21,500 • 13,500	Arabica Robusta (Kouilou)
COLOMBIA • Santa Marta, Cartagena (Atlantic)	12,600 • 10,775	Arabica (Bourbon, Maragogype) • Washed
COSTA RICA • Puerto Limon, Puntarenas,	1,790 • 1,557	Arabica Bourbon • Washed
CUBA • Santiago de Cuba, Havana	450 • 0	Arabica • Washed, some dried
DOMINICAN REPUBLIC • Puerto Plata, Sanchez Barahona, Santo Domingo	850 • 560	Arabica Washed (lavade). Some dried (Corriente)
ECUADOR • Guayaquil, Manta	1,430 • 1,210	Arabica, some Robusta
EL SALVADOR • Acajutla, La Libertad, Cutoco-La Union	2,500 • 2,296	Arabica (19pc Bourbon)
GUADELOUPE * • Pointe-a-Pitre, Basse-Terre		Arabica • Washed and dried
GUATEMALA • Puerto Barrios, Matias de Galvez, San Jose de Guatemala, Santo Tomas	2,600 • 2,275	Arabica (Bourbon and Maragogype); some Robusta

Important Grades	Notes
	Arabica is rich, mellow, delicate acidity. Be certain of Arabica variety. Wide variety of tasts
	Sharp Robusta, mainly for blending in instants.
Robusta, Bugishu	Most Robustas are used as cheap fillers for instant.
Kivu, Ituri.	Robusta used in blending, but Arabica Kivu and Ituri are rich, acid, can add sharpness to mild beans.
Bourbon Santos, Santos, Pie, Flat bean Santos	(See Index for detailed information.)
Manizales, Armenia, Medellin (MAM's); Excelsa, Supreme. Also graded according to size.	
Strictly Hard Bean (SHB) Good Hard Bean (GHB) Medium Hard Bean (MHB) Hard Bean (HB) High Grown Atlantic (HGA) Low Grown Atlantic (LGA)	SHB has fine acidity, good aroma. GHB good body, aroma. HB good acidity, fair aroma and body. HGA limited body aroma. The best beans are among world's finest. SHB and GHB are sharply acid.
	Mainly sold now to Iron Curtain countries. Somewhat akin to lesser Jamaican coffees
Barahonas, Ocoa, Bani	Barahonas good quality, fairly sweet. Others ordinary.
Ecuadors	Sharp flavour, fair body, nearly always blended. World's highest coffee plantations are at Cumbaya (9,000 feet)
Central Strictly High Grown (CSHG); High Grown (HG); Central Standard (CS).	CSHG and HG have good acidity and body. Mild flavour. Lower grade has winey taste.
Extra Prime Semi Hard Bean Hard Bean Strictly Hard Bean Extra Good Washed Prime Good Washed Antigua Coban	Top four growths, going from 3,000-4,500 feet are zesty, sharp, have heavy body and acidity. Others are ordinary. The Antigua and Cobans are rarely seen in Asia or USA, but Europe markets look to them for fine, highly acid, heavy bodies. Superb buys if they can be found.

189

Country • Port(s) of shipping	Total harvested 1980 / 81 • Total exported 1980 / 81 (1000's of 60 kg. Sacks)	Kind of coffee • Drying method
HAITI • Port-au-Prince, Cap Haitien, Les Cayes, Jacmel, Gonaives	485 • 260	Arabica • Dried, 20pc washed
HONDURAS • Puerto Cortes, Ampala	1,265 • 1,153	Arabica • Washed (70pc)
JAMAICA • Kingston	★ ★	Arabica • Washed
NICARAGUA • Corinto, San Juan del Sur	1,050 • 965	Arabica and Maragogype
PANAMA • Cristobal, Balbeo	★ ★	Arabica • Washed
PARAGUAY • Paranagua	75 • 47	Arabica • Washed and dried
PERU • Callao, Matarani, Mollendo	1,100 • 840	Arabica • Washed and unwashed
PUERTO RICO • San Juan	200 • 0	Arabica • Washed
SURINAM • Paramaribe	19 • 0	Liberica • Dried
TRINIDAD AND TOBAGO • Port of Spain	★ ★	Robusta some Arabica • Dried and washed
VENEZUELA • Maracaibo, Puerto Cabello La Guaira, Puerto Sucre	1,073 • 115	Arabica • Washed and dried
MEXICO • Vera Cruz, Coatzacoales, Mazlatan, Puerto Angel, many other ports.	3,600 • 2,200	Arabica • Washed

ASIA

CHINA* • Through Canton		Arabica, Robusta
INDIA • Madras, Mangalore, Tellicherry, Kozhikode, Cochin	2,160 • 1,245	Arabica (65pc) Robusta (35pc)

190

Important Grades	Notes
Strictly High-Grown Washed; High-Grown	"High-Grown" is actually a low 1,500 feet. Pleasant, sweet, usually air-roasted. "Triage" can be either washed or dried, but has many spoiled beans.
Blue Mountain High Mountain Supreme Prime Jamaican Washed	Blue Mountain has the honour of being the highest-priced coffee in the world, and much of it is bought by the Japanese. Regular "Blue Mountain blends" probably have less than ten percent of the real thing. It's very mellow, mild, sweet and aromatic. High Mountain Supreme has medium acidity with good body. Prime Jamaican Washed is fair.
Jinotega; Matagalpa	Mainly used in blends
Chanchamayo	Full-bodied, gently acid.
Puerto Ricans	Delicious, sweet rich — but unless you live in Puerto Rico, or the Vatican (to which it gives an annual gift), you won't find it outside. The coffee is roasted black.
	Only for instant blends
Tachira, Merida, Trujillo, Cucuta, Caracas, Caracas Blue	First three are sometimes marked "Maracaibo". Merida is the most delicate. Caracas and Caracas Blue are delicate and delicious.
Altura (High-Grown); Prima Lavada (High-Washed); Bueno Lavado (Good washed) Specials	Altura versions of the districts below are the best of the different regions; They are all strong with good acidity. Cordobas and Tapachula are light and smooth. Oaxacas and plumas are sharp. Others are risky. A wide choice, but some of the best, as "Specials" are consumed in the country.
Yunan, Hainan	Full-bodied, smokey, sweet, but little is exported. Arabica in Yunan, planted by French. Robusta raised in Hainan.

A. Arabica Plantation A, B, T.
B. Cherry
    Arabica Cherry AB
    Arabica Cherry T
	Plantation coffee has good acidity, body, usually superior to Cherry. Best is from Mysore. "T" means "triage", or spoiled beans.

★ Total of Dahomey, Gabon, Ghana, Guinea and Nigeria: 168 harvested, 100 exported
★ ★ Total of Jamaica, Panama, Trinidad & Tobago, Hawaii: 197 harvested, 87 exported
★ ★ ★ Total from Vietnam, Yemen, New Caledonia, Portuguese Timor; 145 harvested, 89 exported

* Information on some countries not available at publication time

Country • Port(s) of shipping	Total harvested 1980 / 81 • Total exported 1980 / 81 (1000's of 60 kg. Sacks)	Kind of coffee • Drying method
INDONESIA • Sumatra: Medan, Padjant etc Java: Jakarta, Surabaya Bali: Buleleng Celebes: Makassar Timor: Kupang	5,162 • 4,062	Robusta (89pc) Arabica, Liberica
LAOS / VIETNAM • Saigon	★ ★ ★	Arabica
MALAYSIA • Port of Singapore	148 • 0	Arabica (95pc) Robusta, • Dried
PHILIPPINES • Manila	750 • 342	Arabica, Robusta • Dried, some washed
SRI LANKA • Colombo	52 • 43	
THAILAND • Bangkok	Negligible	Arabica
TIMOR • Dili	★ ★ ★	Arabica, Robusta • Washed, dried
YEMEN (PEOPLE'S REPUBLIC OF NORTH YEMEN) • Hodeida, Aden, Mocha	★ ★ ★	Arabica • Dried

PACIFIC

Country • Port(s) of shipping	Total harvested 1980 / 81 • Total exported 1980 / 81 (1000's of 60 kg. Sacks)	Kind of coffee • Drying method
HAWAII • Honolulu	★ ★	Arabica • Washed
NEW CALEDONIA • Noumea	★ ★ ★	Arabica, Robusta • Washed and dried
NEW GUINEA (PAPUA NEW GUINEA) • Lae, Madang	840 • 824	Arabica (90pc) Robusta (10pc)
NEW HEBRIDES * • Espiritu Santo		Robusta • Dried

192

Important Grades	Notes
Labelled by island, but often mislabelled. For Sumatran, insist on Mandheling, Ankola, Bangies.	"Java Arabica" is very rare. The Robustas are good, subtle, mellow. *Kopi luak* is a special rare bean which gets its flavour from being swallowed by small animals which pass it unharmed through the intestines. Most exceptional is Sumatran Arabica. Smooth, heavy, fine flavour, aroma. Superb for drinking black.
	Once was used in strong Thai blends, but recently, little is exported to Asia because of political situation. Some is dark-roasted now in Vietnamese coffee blends, but the original plants grown by French colonials have changed much. In the late 1970's, the Laos were *ordered* to adulterate their coffee with tamarind, in order that the best be exported to Eastern Europe, for foreign exchange.
	Like Indonesian coffees, delicate Robustas, the best coming from Sabah (though frequently smuggled out through the Philippines).
	Until recently, poor blends, but new plantations and experiments are being tried in the South. About 1986, one will know the results.
	Only a few tons exported, but Sri Lanka was the first Asian country to systematically raise coffee and until the blight of 1869 was the most important. Quality not very good today.
	Thailand is the newest member of the International Coffee Organisation, its first coffee having been harvested in 1980. Originally raised in the North Thailand hills, as part of an experimental crop substitute for opium, the coffee has recently been analysed in Switzerland, with exceptionally high marks. Still not available to the outside world (or even in Bangkok), but it should be relatively easy to buy in Chiengmai, Thailand, through the United Nations organisations administering the crop substitution programme.
Timors	Because of political situation very rare to find this delicate coffee on the markets today
Mocha Mocha Extra	Don't confuse this with Ethiopian Mocha: Yemen Mocha, the little available is distinct, piquant, winey, delicious. Best is extra-hard, fine for blending with Java Robusta, creating a smooth brew with real sharpness. Difficult to find in Asia, and in Yemen itself the coffee is horribly weak.
Kona	Production is decreasing, but good Hawaiian coffee is mild smooth, slightly acid with an excellent aroma.
Milds	Rich, pleasant, gaining in popularity.

How to say it

AMHARIC	Bunn	INDONESIAN	Kope
ARABIC	Qahwa	IRANIAN	Gehvé
BASQUE	Kaffia	ITALIAN	Caffé
BRETON	Kafe	JAPANESE	Koohii
BOHEMIAN	Kava	KHMER	Gafé
CANTONESE	Kia-fey	LAOTIAN	Kafe
CZECH	Kava	LATIN	Coffea
DANISH	Kaffé	MALAYAN	Kawa, Koppi
DUTCH	Koffie	MANDARIN	Kafei
EGYPTIAN	Masbout	NORWEGIAN	Kaffé
ESKIMO	Kaufee	POLISH	Kawa
ESPERANTO	Kafo	PORTUGUESE	Café
FINNISH	Kahvi	RUMANIAN	Cafea
FRENCH	Café	RUSSIAN	Kofé
GERMAN	Kaffee	SERBO-CROATIAN	Kafa
GREEK	Kafes	SPANISH	Café
HAWAIIAN	Kopé	SWAHILI	Kahawa
HEBREW	Kavah, Kaffee	TAGALOG	Kapé
HINDI	Coffee	THAI	Kafe
HUNGARIAN	Kavé	TURKISH	Kahvé
		YIDDISH	Kavé

Bibliography

- Allman, T.D. *Rising To Rebellion: Inside El Salvador* (Harper's Magazine, March 1981)
- Blixen, Baroness Karen. *Out Of Africa* (Putnam, London, 1937)
- Brent, Peter, *Far Arabia* (Weidenfeld and Nicholson, London, 1977)
- Brillat-Savarin, Jean-Anthelme, *The Philosopher In The Kitchen* (Penguin, 1970)
- Claiborne, Craig, *Kitchen Primer* (Alfred A. Knopf, 1969)
- Davids, Kenneth, *The Coffee Book* (Whittet Books, 1976)
- Hemphill, Rosemary, *The Penguin Book Of Herbs And Spices* (Penguin, 1979)
- Kolpas, Norman, *The Coffee Lovers' Companion* (Quick Fox, 1977)
- Kritzeck, James, editor, *Anthology of Islamic Literature* (Pelican, 1964)
- Lappe, Frances Moore and Colins, Joseph, *Food First* (Ballantine, 1977)
- Leibowitz, Rene, *The Great Japanese Coffee-House Dream* (Winds, Japan Air Lines, 1979)
- Macmillan, Diane de Lorme, *Coffee Cuisine* (Artists and Writers Publications, 1972)
- Melitta Coffee Group, Germany: Numerous publications
- Ministry External Affairs, Brazil: *Brazil: Resources And Possibilities* (Brazilian Ministry of External Affairs, 1976)
- Muir, Frank: *The Frank Muir Book* (William Heinemann, 1976)
- Pankhurst, Richard, editor: *Travellers In Ethiopia* (Oxford University Press, 1960)
- Price, Pamela Vandyke, *The Penguin Book Of Spirits And Liqueurs* (Penguin, 1979)
- Roden, Claudia, *A Book Of Middle Eastern Food* (Penguin 1968)
- Roden, Claudia, *Coffee* (Penguin, 1977)
- Roden, Claudia, *The World Of Coffee* (Sunday Times, London)
- Schapira, Joel, David and Karl, *The Book Of Coffee And Tea* (St. Martin's Press, 1973)
- Schweitzer, Albert, *J.S. Bach* (A and C Black, 1964)
- Starbird, Ethel, *The Bonanza Bean, Coffee* (National Geographic Magazine, March 1981)
- Sutherland, James, editor, *The Oxford Book Of Literary Anecdotes* (Pocket Books, 1976)
- Thesiger, Wilfred, *Arabian Sands* (Longmans, Green, 1959)
- Twain, Mark, *The Innocents Abroad* (Signet, 1966)
- Ullendorff, Edward, *The Ethiopians* (Oxford University Press, 1960)
- Wallechinsky, David etc, *The Book Of Lists* (William Morrow, 1977)
- Wattenberg, Ben and Smith, Ralph Lee, *The New Nations of Africa* (Hart, 1963)
- Wise, Donald, editor, *Asia 1982 Yearbook* (Far Eastern Economic Review, 1982)

List of plates

Index